The Conspiracy of Feelings
by Yurii Olesha

and

The Little Theatre of the Green Goose
by Konstanty Ildefons Gałczyński

Routledge Harwood Polish and East European Theatre Archive
A series of books edited by Daniel Gerould, Graduate School, City University of New York, USA

Volume 1
To Steal a March on God
Hanna Krall
Translated and with an introduction by Jadwiga Kosicka

Volume 2
Alternative Theatre in Poland
1954–1989
Kathleen Cioffi

Volume 3
Country House
Stanisław Ignacy Witkiewicz
Translated and with an introduction by Daniel Gerould

Volume 4
The Trap
Tadeusz Różewicz
Translated by Adam Czerniawski

Volume 5
Polish Romantic Drama
Harold B. Segal

Volume 6
The Mannequins' Ball
Bruno Jasienski
Translated and with an introduction by Daniel Gerould

Volume 7
Leading Creators in Twentieth-Century Czech Theatre
Jarka Burian

Volume 8
Encounters with Tadeusz Kantor
Krzysztof Miklaszewski
Edited and translated by George Hyde

Volume 9
Ireneusz Iredyński: Selected one-act plays for radio
Edited by Kevin Windle

Please see the back of this book for other titles in the Routledge Harwood Polish and East European Theatre Archive series

The Conspiracy of Feelings
by Yurii Olesha

and

The Little Theatre of the Green Goose
by Konstanty Ildefons Gałczyński

Edited by
Daniel Gerould

LONDON AND NEW YORK

First published 2002
by Routledge

Published 2014 by Routledge
2 Park Square, Milton Park, Abingdon, Oxfordshire OX14 4RN

Simultaneously published in the
USA and Canada by Routledge
711 Third Avenue, New York, NY, 10017, USA

First issued in paperback 2015

Routledge is an imprint of the Taylor & Francis Group, an informa business

© 2002 Taylor & Francis

Typeset by EXPO Holdings

All rights reserved. No part of this book may be reprinted or reproduced or utilised in any form or by any electronic, mechanical, or other means, now known or hereafter invented, including photocopying and recording, or in any information storage or retrieval system, without permission in writing from the publishers.

British Library Cataloguing in Publication Data
A catalogue record for this book is available from the British Library

Library of Congress Cataloging in Publication Data
Olesha, IUrii Karlovich, 1899–1960.
    [Zagovor chuvstv. English]
    The conspiracy of feelings / by Yurii Olesha. And The Little Theatre of the Green Goose / by Konstanty Ildefons Gałczyński; [both] edited by Daniel Gerould.
    p. cm. – (Routledge Harwood Polish and East European Theatre Archive ; 10)
    Translated by Daniel Gerould.
    1. Slavic drama – 20th century – Translations into English. I. Gerould, Daniel Charles, 1928– II. Gałczyński, Konstanty Ildefons. Teatrzyk "Zielona Geś" ma zaszczyt przedstawic. English. III. Title: Little Theatre of the Green Goose. IV. Title. V. Series.

PG551.E5 O44 2002
891.72`42–dc21

2001048500

ISBN13: 978-0-415-86635-4 (pbk)
ISBN13: 978-0-415-27504-0 (hbk)

Contents

Introduction to the series	vii
List of Plates	ix
Introduction to *The Conspiracy of Feelings* Daniel Gerould	1
Note on the Text and the Translation of *The Conspiracy of Feelings*	11
The Conspiracy of Feelings by Yurii Olesha Translated by Daniel Gerould	13
Appendix	
"The Author About His Play"	57
"Notes of a Dramatist"	59
Alternate Ending to *The Conspiracy of Feelings*	65
Anatolii Lunacharsky on *The Conspiracy of Feelings*	66
Mariya O. Knebel on A. D. Popov: Director, Teacher, Friend	69
Selective Bibliography	71
Introduction to *The Little Theatre of the Green Goose* Daniel Gerould	73
The Little Theatre of the Green Goose by Konstanty Ildefons Gałczyński Translated by Daniel Gerould	75

Introduction to the Series

The *Routledge Harwood Polish and East European Theatre Archive* makes available in English translation major works of Poland's dramatic literature as well as monographs and critical studies on Polish and East European playwrights, theatre artists and stage history. Although emphasis is placed on the contemporary period, the archive also encompasses the ninteenth-century roots of modern theatre practice in Romanticism and Symbolism. The individual plays will contain authoritative introductions that place the works in their historical and theatrical contexts.

Daniel Gerould

List of Plates

The plates follow page 55.
1. Ivan Babichev – A. Goryunov. Vakhtangov Theatre 1929
2. Shapiro – B. Shchukin. Vakhtangov Theatre, 1929
3. Valya – E. Alekseeva. Vakhtangov Theatre, 1929
4. *The Conspiracy of Feelings:* Scene 2 – the communal kitchen. Directed by Aleksi Popov, designed by Nikolai Akimov. Vakhtangov Theatre, 1929
5. *The Conspiracy of Feelings:* Scene 3 – Ivan and Andrei Babichev (O. Galzunov). Vakhtangov Theatre, 1929
6. *The Conspiracy of Feelings:* Scene 3 – Andrei Babichev (O. Glazunov), Valya (E. Alekseeva) Vakhtangov Theatre, 1929
7. *The Conspiracy of Feelings:* Scene 4 – Ivan, Valya, Shapiro, Andrei, Vakhtangov Theatre, 1929
8. *The Conspiracy of Feelings:* Scene 5 – Kavalerov's dream. Kavalerov – V. Moskin. Vakhtagov Theatre, 1929
9. *The Conspiracy of Feelings:* Scene 6 – the Name Day Party, Vaktangov Theatre, 1929
10. *The Conspiracy of Feelings*: Scene 7 – the Stadium. Vakhtangov Theatre, 1929

Introduction to *The Conspiracy of Feelings*
Daniel Gerould

In 1927 Yurii Olesha (1899–1960) published his short novel *Envy* about the struggle between the old and new in Soviet society. Full of wit and irony and written in a dazzling metaphoric style, it was the literary sensation of the year. The Vakhtangov theatre asked Olesha to adapt *Envy* for the stage. The play, called *The Conspiracy of Feelings*, was not a simple adaptation, but an original work that reconceived the novel, omitting certain characters and episodes and adding others; it received two spectacular premieres in 1929 and became one of the most celebrated and controversial Soviet productions of the period between the wars.

In his short essay, "The Author about His Play," which appeared just before opening night in Leningrad, Olesha explained that the theme of the work was the battle for passionate commitment. Would the contest be won by the obsolete intellectual, Nikolai Kavalerov, or by the crass but heroic communist sausage maker, Andrei Babichev? The real question is: what was the author's own commitment?

The Conspiracy of Feelings explores the precarious position of the intelligentsia in the new collective state, a subject for which the playwright drew upon his own experiences. "I want to transform myself," Olesha confessed with characteristic slyness. "Of course, I'm uncomfortable ... being an intellectual. ... It is a weakness I'd like to overcome."

As portrayed in *The Conspiracy of Feelings*, the successful proletarian revolution of 1917, so ardently sought by the radical bourgeoisie, has created a world in which intellectuals have no place. Andrei's brother, Ivan, and his disciple Kavalerov are the "superfluous men" of the new era, descendants of the "superfluous" heroes of nineteenth-century Russian literature, who were isolated and cut off from productive lives by the oppressive Tsarist regime. The alienated intelligentsia remains as alienated in the communist technological society as under capitalism, and for much the same reasons. The new socialist order is mechanized and impersonal, with no place for the individual.

Before 1917, hope for the intelligentsia lay in exaggerated expectations of a revolutionary world still to be born. Now in the disillusion of the post-natal period, there can only be futile longing for a former way of life already doomed to destruction and the absurd dream of reinstating violent passions capable of subverting the well-ordered and policed Marxist-Leninist state. Under Ivan's leadership, the old feelings of greed, jealousy, and lust – despicable, but at least human – are enlisted in a conspiracy, an abortive counter-revolution against the mechanized communist utopia with its mass-production kitchens and bedrooms.

The title, *The Conspiracy of Feelings*, locates the play in an enduring Russian tradition of "conspiracies" and of seeing conspiracy everywhere. The Russian Revolution had operated as a conspiracy when it was forced to work underground, and once triumphant, it incorporated conspiratorial techniques in its system of governance. The Stalinist system maintained itself through accusations of conspiracy against everyone. A number of plays in the 1920s, 30s, and 40s adopted the word as part of the title: Alexei Tolstoi's *Conspiracy of the Empress* (1924), Mikhail Levidov's *Conspiracy of Equals* (1928) – about Babeuf's uprising under the directory, as is Ilya Ehrenburg's novel of the same title – and Nikolai Virta's *Conspiracy of the Condemned* (1948). Sergei Eisenstein subtitled the second part of *Ivan the Terrible* "conspiracy of the boyars;" the expression, "conspiracy of silence" – coined in 1820 to describe moral cowardice under Nicholas I – was used to characterize the ubiquitous fear and apathy in the face of Stalinism; and Bruno Jasieński conceived the idea of a "conspiracy of the indifferent" (the title of his last unfinished novel) to depict the new automated mentality of the 1930s.

The premieres of *The Conspiracy of Feelings* at Moscow's Vakhtangov Theatre (March 13, 1929) and at Leningrad's Bolshoi Dramatic Theatre (December 28, 1929) were greeted with enthusiastic reviews and praise for the play's brilliance, but bewilderment at the work's ideological intent. Party critics wrote voluminously about the troubling ambiguity of the author's attitude toward his characters. Although all agreed that the play incisively exposed the malice and pettiness of the dying bourgeois world, there was shrill debate as to whether or not Andrei Babichev was truly a "positive hero," a concept soon to become a shibboleth in the theory of socialist realism.

According to Olesha, who was quickly put on the defensive, Andrei was to be taken as the heroic new man, and the director of the production at the Vakhtangov Theatre, Alexei Popov, called him a "poet of utilitarianism" built on the scale of Lenin. The cultured intellectual

Anatolii Lunacharsky, People's Commissar for Education, who tried to keep the Soviet theatre pluralistic during the 1920s, defended the play, arguing that Andrei was not an idealized figure abstractly representing everything a good communist should be, but rather a particular dramatic figure in a play. Other more tendentious Marxist-Leninists condemned Andrei as a crypto-capitalist wheeler-dealer in the American style who believed that making salami was more important than building socialism. In the lobby of the Bolshoi Dramatic Theatre in Leningrad, the model of a new mass-production kitchen which could serve up to 15,000 meals per day prompted one critic to observe that this exhibit was a more convincing example of the triumph of the new collective way of life than Andrei Babichev and the entire drama.

Despite the critical polemics, Olesha's play was popular with audiences. The Vakhtangov production played in repertory 94 times over a period of two years. There were also highly successful productions at the Workers Theatre in Tiflis in 1930, at the Dramatic Theatre in Samara in 1931, and at other regional theatres.

In the increasingly repressive 1930s, *The Conspiracy of Feelings* was condemned as false to Soviet reality in suggesting that the individual would be sacrificed to the mass. And since it did not conform to the tenets of socialist realism – the newly proclaimed dogma – the work was denounced as decadent, grotesque, and expressionistic in form.

Although the play was printed in the Leningrad newspaper *Krasnaya Gazeta* a few days after the premiere, *The Conspiracy of Feelings* did not appear in book form during the author's lifetime, nor was it revived on the stage after 1931. Following Stalin's death Olesha's works were reissued, but another fifteen years passed before *The Conspiracy* was published for the first time in a collection of Olesha's plays in 1968.

Once the play is removed from the narrow sphere of partisan polemics, it can be seen to treat all points of view ironically. Olesha's great accomplishment is to show the struggle of old and new in Soviet life not didactically, but polyphonically and irreverently, reducing the conflict to the level of slapstick comedy and clowning. Not surprisingly, recent interpreters of Olesha find that the concepts of the carnivalesque and the dialogic, developed by his contemporary and fellow Odessan, Mikhail Bakhtin, applies to the special sensibility of *Envy* and *The Conspiracy of Feelings*.

Whatever his personal views, as a playwright Olesha practiced the dialogic by refusing to take sides among the competing voices of his protagonists, and he emulated carnival's disrespectful overturning of received hierarchies. "The circus is the basis of my life," the author declared, "Of all spectacles I loved the circus the most." Eschewing ideological rhetoric in favor of stunts and gags, Olesha mocks both bourgeois man's ineffectual anguish and socialist man's foolish arrogance.

The Russian theatrical avant-garde had already established a carnivalesque tradition in the staging of the classics. Meyerhold had experimented with acrobatics in his famous production of Ostrovsky's *The Forest* in 1922. The following year, Eisenstein turned Ostrovsky's *Enough Stupidity in Every Wise Man* into a circus and clown show. These productions, however, played against the texts of classical works. Olesha incorporated into the fabric of his play elements of Meyerhold's theatricalism, uniting striking visual images and clowning with the more traditional verbal structure. Alexei Popov's direction and Nikolai Akimov's sets for the production at the Vakhtangov Theatre powerfully evoked carnivalesque eccentricity and profanation.

Olesha undercuts tragedy and seriousness at every moment. The time of heroism and greatness is past. Ivan and Kavalerov offer jealousy, envy, spite, and petty violence as the only alternatives to Soviet stability. The third Babichev brother, Roman, the true revolutionary who was executed for throwing a bomb, might seem to be a correct index of the heroic gesture, but as Andrei's sidekick, Shapiro, points out, anyone can throw a bomb, whereas it takes great skill to make a good salami. The only possible insurrection left is a counter-revolution on the sexual level, an absurd conspiracy of ineffectual malcontents.

In his "Notes of a Dramatist" (1933), Olesha laments that the Soviet system has taken away from playwrights two of the principal motive forces of Western drama: guns and money. Under the new regime fortune hunting and inheritance seeking can no longer be primary mechanisms of plot. And the impossibility of private ownership of weapons has rid the stage of the gunfire, which even in Chekhov was the chief means of bringing a play to an end.

To win the recent revolutionary struggles and civil war shooting the class enemy was essential, but once the ideal workers state is established, firearms are no longer needed or allowed. The new society has been purified of violence as well as violent emotions. Because the guns of rebellion have been confiscated, the weapons of combat in *The Conspiracy of Feelings* become Shakespeare versus salami – an unequal battle, since the salami maker has appropriated Shakespearean imagery for his sausage salesmanship.

Common everyday objects become the weapons in this new warfare: Kavalerov wields his razor, Andrei his basin, Ivan his pillow. The revolutionary battles of the past have turned into a pillow fight among clowns; heroic combat has become organized sports. Stifled and embittered, Ivan eggs others on to senseless personal violence as the only possible form of social rebellion.

For Olesha, as novelist and story writer, metaphor is the magical device, which, like Viktor Shklovsky's "defamiliarization," enables the writer to rediscover wonder in the face of the world. And in *The Conspiracy of Feelings*, there are many brilliant verbal metaphors, such as Ivan's description of himself: "The bags under my eyes hang down like violet stockings." But Olesha the playwright adapts literary metaphor to the stage in the form of visual theatrical images. Ivan's pillow, for example, becomes an embodiment of the play's central themes. Valya used to sleep on the dirty yellow pillow Ivan totes about with him. Once redolent of childhood and the past, it has now become shabby and smelly.

The pillow is an accessory to love-making and a passport to sleep, dreaming, and the unconscious, which play major roles in *The Conspiracy of Feelings*. Kavalerov (a man from the past, a "cavalier") is looking for a place to sleep and dream his dreams of romance and glory; Andrei and Annichka each provide him with a bed. It is on Annichka's giant bed that we see his dream unfold before our eyes.

At the name-day party all the characters divulge their innermost dreams and desires under the influence of Ivan's sacred relic, the pillow. Ivan regards beds as holy, the source of the inner personal life that he wishes to preserve inviolate. Andrei centers his attack on the home and family; he wishes to demystify the bedroom and mechanize the sleeping and sexual acts performed there.

Ivan's derby – "rusty-brown with age" and looking like a Russian Easter cake – is the obsolete badge of honor of bankers or business men. In the new society derbies are worn only by old-clothes peddlers; Ivan is such a junk man, hawking his scraps of old emotions collected here and there in his travels about the city, darting in and out of squalid apartment buildings. In contrast to Ivan's derby is Andrei's sparkling basin, so cleansed and polished that it brightly reflects the outside world.

For Andrei, water is most beautiful when it is in the basin, reflecting the window rather than flowing freely. His goal is to order and render existence secure in the new era by restraining and controlling the free flow of life. Both Ivan and Kavalerov fear Andrei's appropriation of Valya as a reservoir, an artificially contained body of water for use by the community. For whom will she be an incubator or breeder – the old world or the new?

Valya is the fluid feminine element in the play which the three principal male characters wish to utilize for their own purposes. Valya is the last hope of salvation for Ivan and Kavalerov, a life-force free of politics, essential for continuing the race. Ivan does not want her to have children for the new era and thereby to continue it. Kavalerov hopes to continue the old world by winning Valya. Ivan and Kavalerov see the containment of emotions, like the confinement of water, as enslavement to reason; freely flowing water suggests all the subjective feelings and uncontrolled emotions.

Like the novel *Envy*, *The Conspiracy of Feelings* flows like water. Its structure is loose, consisting of seven disconnected episodes linked thematically. Plot as a logical, linear sequence of events has been discarded. Less the imitation of an action than a variety of images expressing opposing attitudes to a central problem, the play is a "debating match," to use Olesha's own formulation of his dramatic technique.

Although *The Conspiracy of Feelings* makes extensive use of visual theatrical images, it effectively employs traditional literary devices as well. Prominent among these are ironic Biblical parallels and allusions. Ivan, likened to Christ, proves to be a false prophet, who offers murder instead of salvation. A miracle worker, his wonders always miscarry. Intruding into a wedding, he reverses the marriage of Cana by turning wine into water. He inverts Christ's advice to turn the other cheek and forgive the woman taken in adultery by urging the young man to kill the husband – another ironic reversal since normally it would be the husband's role to punish or forgive the lover. At the name-day party (which Lunacharsky called Ivan's Last Supper), a further ironic reversal occurs: whereas Judas kissed Christ, Ivan, the Christ figure, kisses Kavalerov; but just as Judas was responsible for Christ's death, it is Kavalerov who is responsible for killing Ivan.

Olesha provides three possible conclusions to his story. The ending of the novel *Envy* is inconclusive. Kavalerov does not murder Ivan but simply lives as before, caught between two worlds and unable to act. After a drunken binge, Kavalerov adopts what Ivan claims is the greatest of all emotions, indifference. Ivan and Kavalerov will take turns sleeping with Annichka. As the novel draws to a close, it is Kavalerov's turn. No one has gained a decisive victory.

In the first version of the play that Olesha drafted, Kavalerov comes to the sports stadium in order to kill Andrei, but upon catching sight of Valya, drops his razor and slumps to the ground inertly. Ivan declares that Kavalerov should be put on display in a museum, but Andrei orders them both to be taken off as the soccer match begins. As in the novel, no one is killed, and nothing is decided. The Moscow edition of Olesha's plays published in 1968 prints this version.

During the rehearsals at the Vakhtangov Theatre Olesha worked out a new, more definitive ending for *The Conspiracy of Feelings*, which was used for all subsequent productions. Until the last moment, it appears that Kavalerov will kill Andrei, but suddenly realizing that he has wasted his life by following a false prophet, he turns the razor not on Andrei, but on Ivan, thereby murdering his own past. As the football players come down the ramp, Andrei declares, "That's the end of the old passions ... The new world is beginning."

This denouement constitutes a surprising reversal that could scarcely have been anticipated, but that brings the play to a theatrically swift and ironic conclusion. Thematically, however, it offers no resolution, as Valery Kirpotin, a hostile party critic, correctly observed:

> The denouement of the play is Kavalerov's blow with the razor. Kavalerov kills Ivan Babichev and thus seems to resolve the conflict between the two Babichev brothers in favor of Andrei. But the denouement is false. ... It is no culmination, and it does not solve the conflict within the play. ... Kavalerov could just as easily have killed Andrei Babichev, and then the conflict would have been decided in favor of Ivan Babichev.

Olesha's ambivalence – about his play, about his characters, about himself – runs deep. "Hamletism," a long-standing Russian obsession with intellectual irresolution, lies at the heart of *The Conspiracy of Feelings*, in which references to Shakespeare abound.

Olesha uses Shakespeare as parody, subtext, image, and allusion. Kavalerov's two possessions, when he arrives at Andrei's, are his razor and his volume of Shakespeare. Shakespeare's name appears in nonsensical exchanges between Valya, Kavalerov, Shapiro, and Andrei. *Othello* serves as ironic comparison for two love triangles: Ivan-Valya-Kavalerov and the Young Man-Lizaveta-the Husband. The provincial governor killed by Roman Babichev's bomb is likened to Othello, governor-general of Cyprus.

But it is *Hamlet* which provides the most complete analog to *The Conspiracy of Feelings*. Ophelia, the name of Ivan's anti-machine, is appropriated by Andrei for the name of his salami, just as Valya herself, linked with the salami, is appropriated by him. Ophelia, at her father's command, rejects Hamlet; so Valya spurns Kavalerov.

Kavalerov, the Hamlet of *The Conspiracy of Feelings*, must act as avenger of the nineteenth century. Throughout the play, the major opposition is between the introspective and intellectual Hamlet-like dreamer Kavalerov and the Fortinbras-like strong man Andrei. In the final scene, in a crucial speech not present in the novel, Ivan makes these identifications explicit, proclaiming the entrance of Fortinbras-Andrei, who cares nothing for the anguish and passions of Hamlet-Kavalerov.

In Eastern Europe, where the vicissitudes of history and power politics have borne down particularly hard on intellectuals and dreamers, the opposition between Hamlet and Fortinbras assumes an importance it never has had in the West. Fortinbras, who appears twice in *Hamlet* and speaks a total of twenty-seven lines, becomes the Prince's chief foil – the strong man versus the indecisive intellectual – and ultimately overshadows him. Olesha was the first to use this analog as the basis for an original play.

Other Eastern European writers walk this line. In modern Polish literature, for example, the opposition Hamlet-Fortinbras is the subject of Zbigniew Herbert's "Elegy for Fortinbras," and it serves as the underlying structure for Mrożek's *Tango*, Żurek's *After Hamlet*, and Głowacki's *Fortinbras Gets Drunk*.

Because of his ambiguous attitude to the new order, Olesha remained suspected of Hamletism. In his address to the First Congress of Soviet Writers in 1934, he tried to answer the charge that Kavalerov was an autobiographical portrait.

> Yes, Kavalerov did look at the world through my eyes. Kavalerov's colors, lights, ages, comparisons, metaphors and thoughts about things were mine.

But the writer went on to defend his imaginative identification of himself with Kavalerov against the accusation made by literary critics that Kavalerov was worthless and useless. In response, he claimed the right of an author to utilize his own vision based on his own experiences of the world and explained that he could not write about revolutionary heroes and workers on construction sites implementing the First Five Year Plan. He said that he must write from his own convictions and experience; he was born into the old world but would try to create a bridge to the new world by being true to the impressions of his youth which would reach the youth of the present.

Despite this attempt to find a way of not feeling useless and unwanted, Olesha's career as a major creative writer was virtually over; he adopted a position of relative silence and perhaps the greatest emotion of all (according to Ivan Babichev), indifference, in order to weather the storm of the Stalinist era. He died peacefully and quietly in 1960.

After the seemingly irreversible triumph of the Bolshevik Revolution, Olesha could scarcely have imagined that Ivan and Kavalerov's sexual counter-revolution had any chance of success against the Soviet juggernaut. But with the unexpected demise of the Soviet Union paradoxical reversals have occurred. Olesha's satire has lost none of its sting. In post-communist Russia, the ideals of both the Babichev brothers appear to be flourishing. The hucksterism and entrepreneurial flamboyance displayed by the sausage salesman, Andrei, go hand in hand with the tawdry greed and lust hawked by Ivan, "king of vulgarians." And the gunfire and fortune-hunting, which Olesha thought had been forever eradicated in the workers utopia, have made a strong comeback. Only the ideals of the intellectual Kavalerov still appear destined to defeat.

Ultimately, Olesha's satire resonates beyond boundaries of politics and nationality. The topsy-turvy world of *The Conspiracy of Feelings*, with its sports marketing, its selling of products through association with famous names of artists and revolutionaries, and its fantastic anti-machine machine designed to subvert the spread of technology, seems surprisingly familiar.

Note on the Text and on the Translation of *The Conspiracy of Feelings*
Daniel Gerould

The Conspiracy of Feelings (*Zagovor Chuvstv*) was performed in Moscow at the Vakhtangov Theatre on March 13, 1929, and first published in 1968 in Russian and in English (in an earlier version of this translation: *Drama and Theatre*, VII [Fall, 1968]).

The translation is based on the typescript in the Moscow Theatre Museum Library, which I copied by hand in the Spring of 1967. The Russian text, which appears to be the one used in the Vakhtangov production, differs from the version that appears in the first edition of Olesha's plays published in Moscow in 1968. The differences are for the most part slight, mainly a reduction in the length of long speeches, except in Scene 6 and particularly Scene 7 where the changes are substantive. In Scene 6, the Name Day Party, the order of speeches and the names of the characters sometimes diverge. I discuss the two different endings in the Introduction, and the earlier denouement is included in the Appendix.

The titles given each of the seven scenes first appeared on the posters and in the programs for the Vakhtangov production.

The Conspiracy of Feelings
A Play in Four Acts and Seven Scenes
by
Yurii Olesha
Translated by Daniel Gerould

All inquiries concerning performance rights of *The Conspiracy of Feelings* should be addressed to: Samuel French, 45 West 25th St., New York, NY 10010, USA

Characters

ANDREI PETROVICH BABICHEV (Director of the Food Industry Trust)
IVAN (his brother)
NIKOLAI KAVALEROV
VALYA (Ivan's adopted daughter)
SOLOMON DAVIDOVICH SHAPIRO
ANNICHKA PROKOPOVICH
LIZAVETA IVANOVNA
A YOUNG MAN (her lover)
HER HUSBAND
TENANTS
DOCTOR (in the dream)
A WOMAN CELEBRATING HER NAME DAY
ZINOCHKA
LADY IN GREEN
VIC
A VENERABLE OLD MAN
A LESS VENERABLE OLD MAN
A VERY DRUNK GUEST
A LESS DRUNK GUEST
MIKHAIL MIKHAILYCH
HARMAN (a German)
FESSENKOV
WAITERS, SPECTATORS, TENANTS

The action takes place in Moscow, 1928.

Act I: Scene 1
"Why Did You Kill Andrei Babichev?"

(*In* ANDREI BABICHEV's *house. Morning. A light, clean room. On the wall, in a glass frame, a plan of the mass-production kitchen, "The Quarter." The huge legend "The Quarter" hits you in the eye. First floor. Windows, glass door, with a terrace visible behind them, greenery, a garden. Very light and bright. Doors to the right and to the left.* KAVALEROV *sits on a messy bed made up on the sofa. He gets dressed slowly. On the floor in the middle of the room, a mat with a stool standing on it.* ANDREI BABICHEV *pours water out of a pitcher into a basin.* ANDREI *is stripped to the waist, in knitted underwear.*)

KAVALEROV: A month ago you came up to me as I was coming out of a bar. You took me home with you even though I was just a nobody. I'm only a poor working man and for a month now I've been living in a famous man's house.
ANDREI: Don't be so modest. Everything's been going all right. You know English. I'm working on a book and you're a great deal of help. I'm very grateful to you.
KAVALEROV: That means I'll be able to sleep on this sofa until you finish your book. Right? And then what?
ANDREI: Then, I don't know ...
KAVALEROV: Well, if that's the case ... I'll leave today.
ANDREI: It's not right to quit your job, is it now? No, it isn't. (*He puts the basin on the stool.*) It's a terrific basin. If you ask me, water looks much better in a basin than flowing freely. See how blue the basin is. That's real beauty. There's the window over there, and if you bend over you can see how the window dances in the basin. (*He bends over the basin and looks into it, standing in front of it.*) Boy, that's really great. (*He jiggles the basin.*) Well, now. (*Admiringly.*) That's real beauty. (*He goes into the bedroom.*)
KAVALEROV (*alone*): How much do you weigh?
ANDREI (*from the bedroom*): 216. (*He comes out with a towel in his hands.*) Yesterday, as I was going downstairs, all of a sudden I felt something weird – my breasts were shaking. Get that, Kavalerov. My breasts were shaking like an old woman's. It was revolting. I decided to start a new series of exercises. (*He starts exercising. Squatting positions.*) O-o-one. You ought to do exercises. O-o-one, two-o ... You'll get fat ... How old are you, Kavalerov?
KAVALEROV: 28 ... I'm as old as the twentieth century.
ANDREI: (*extending and pulling back his arms*): Ah, two, ah, two, ah, ah, ah, ah, two.

KAVALEROV: I often think about the twentieth century. This century of ours is an illustrious one. I've grown up with this century.

ANDREI: Ah, two, ah, two, ah, two. Phew! ... (*Running in place.*) Op-pop, op-pop, op-pop ...

KAVALEROV: In Europe, there are many opportunities for a talented person to become famous. There an individual can achieve personal fame. But here? Here they don't like personal fame. Isn't that right?

ANDREI: That's right. (*He lies on his back. He raises first one leg, then the other.*)

KAVALEROV: In our country all the paths of glory are blocked by barriers. A talented person either grows dull or else has to raise the barrier by causing an uproar.

ANDREI (*raises his leg*): Ouch! O-one. My leg's like a barrier. One leg weighs 100 pounds.

KAVALEROV: You say that personal glory has to disappear. You say that the individual is nothing, and only the masses exist. That's what you say.

ANDREI: That's what we say.

KAVALEROV: Rubbish. I want my own personal glory ... I demand some recognition. (ANDREI, *raising himself on tiptoe, goes down on his hands and knees in such a way that he turns his rear end toward* KAVALEROV.) It's easy enough for you to show me your rear end.

ANDREI (*on his feet again*): Phew ... that does it. Now for some water. How about a little water?

KAVALEROV: You insist on a sober approach to things and to life in general. So I'm going to create something obviously absurd just for its own sake. I'll do something crazy and original ... Just for its own sake. You want everything to be purposeful, but I want to be purposeless. (*A pause.*) I'll go hang myself on your front porch. (*At this point* ANDREI *goes out the door to the right, taking the basin with him, then returns.*)

ANDREI (*coming back*): Better hang yourself in front of the Commissariat of the National Economy. In Varvarskaya Square. There's a huge arch there. You've seen it. It'll really be impressive there. (ANDREI *goes out the door to the right again, taking the stool out with him.*)

KAVALEROV (*alone*): Stupid bureaucrat. (ANDREI *returns, goes into the bedroom through the door on the left. To* ANDREI *in the bedroom.*) I want to tell you about a little incident.

ANDREI (*from the bedroom*): Tell me about a little incident.

KAVALEROV: Once ... it was a long time ago ... I was a schoolboy. My father took me to the museum where they have wax figures. You know, the wax works exhibition? You know, there are those glass cases. And they have figures in them. Cleopatra. A gorilla kidnaping a young girl. Robespierre on the guillotine. There was a handsome man lying in one of these cases. He was wearing a tail-coat. He was wounded in the chest. He was dying, his eyelids were closing. My father said to me: That's the French President Sadi Carnot. He's been wounded by an anarchist. (*A pause.*) Such a wonderful man lying there with his beard sticking straight up in the air. His life was slowly passing by, like the hours on a clock. It was wonderful. It was then that I first heard the roar of time.

ANDREI (*from the bedroom*): What?

KAVALEROV: The roar of time ... Do you understand? I heard how time sounds. Understand? Time rushed over me. I cried for joy. I decided to become famous.

ANDREI: Yeah, yeah.

KAVALEROV: That was the day I made up my mind to become famous. I decided at all costs to make sure that someday my image and wax double filled with the sound of the ages would also stand in splendor in the great museum of the future. (ANDREI *comes out of the bedroom dressed.*) There are people that things don't like and people that things do like. That's you Andrei Petrovich. Things like you. Everything looks stylish on you. But things don't like me. (ANDREI *has taken food from the small cupboard. Sits down at the round table, eats.*) The furniture tries to trip me. Yesterday the corner of this desk (*Points to the corner of the desk.*) actually bit me. Look, I just dropped my collar button. Where is it? Where did it disappear to? If you drop your collar button, it'll turn up right at your feet. But my collar button's rolled under the sofa. Look, the sofa's laughing at me.

ANDREI: Kavalerov, you should meet my brother, Ivan, you'd have a lot in common. By the way, my brother Ivan has turned up again in Moscow. He hasn't shown up for a whole year. My brother Ivan's all over the place, and then suddenly he disappears. Where's Ivan? Nobody knows. It's anybody's guess whether he's in prison or an insane asylum. (*A pause.*) Yesterday my brother was walking along Petrovsky Boulevard. I saw him from the bus stop. He was walking along holding a pillow by one of the corners. And there were children running after him. The nut ... He just kept walking on and on, then he stopped, took off his derby, and bowed in all directions.

KAVALEROV: With a pillow?

ANDREI: With a pillow. He's quite a nut, my brother Ivan.

KAVALEROV: Why does he go around with a pillow?

ANDREI: Oh, the hell with him. (*A pause.* KAVALEROV *sits down and shaves. He continues shaving during the rest of the scene.*) Well, Kavalerov, we're about to witness some great events ...

KAVALEROV: Because your brother's turned up ...

ANDREI: Oh, the hell with my brother. What I'm talking about is the new kind of salami we're going to put on the market in a few days.

KAVALEROV: For a whole month I've been hearing about nothing but that salami ...

ANDREI: I suppose you think it's so easy to make salami? And such a salami, too ... Do you understand anything about the salami business?

KAVALEROV: Not a thing.

ANDREI (*he's finished eating, and feels great*): It's going to be a sensational salami. You should have some respect for me, Kavalerov. I've achieved amazing results. It'll be a great triumph. You'll see ... Ho-ho ... it'll be terrific. We're going to send it to the exhibition in Milan. And then we'll get down to work on "The Quarter." (*He goes up to the map of "The Quarter," looks at it, steps back, draws near again, admires it.*) Kavalerov, we're going to call our mass-production kitchen "The Quarter." That's great. If you ask me, that's great. "The Quarter," mass-production kitchen. And why call it "The Quarter"? Because the two-course dinner will sell for 25 kopecks. For a quarter. Great, eh? And they'll both be meat courses! If you ask me, that's great. Look at the plan the German drew up ... It's a beauty. The building's gigantic. The garden's over here. See? There are the towers and a small square ... Terrific, isn't it? If you ask me, it's terrific. That German really knows his stuff ... And there's your "Quarter" ... the all-purpose cafeteria. Breakfast, snacks, dinner, home delivery, baby food, scientifically-prepared cream of wheat. You know, Kavalerov, we'll be serving 2,000 dinners a day. A sea of cabbage soup ... You ought to write an epic about it, Kavalerov.

KAVALEROV: About what?

ANDREI: About cabbage soup. An epic about dinner on a grand scale. 2,000 people eating cabbage soup to the strains of Wagner. If you ask me, that's great. An epic about the abolition of sauce pans. (*A pause.*) It'll be terrific ... just terrific ... To hell with half-pound boxes and little bottles, to hell with tiny packages ... Just think of it: a half-pound of salt, a half-pint of cooking oil ... it's revolting ... it's so primitive ... We'll build "The Quarter," then you'll see ... 100 gallons of cooking oil ... I'll bash in those pots and pans and smash all those little bottles ... to hell with them all.

KAVALEROV: Andrei Petrovich, you know what? I think I saw your brother yesterday too. He looks like you.

ANDREI: He does ... but he's a little shorter.

KAVALEROV: He was wearing a derby.

ANDREI: He always wears a derby. I'd like to bash in that pot of his too. The nut. In a derby. The monkey ... In this country it's not right to wear a derby. In this country only rag pickers or ambassadors wear derbies ...

KAVALEROV: But he was. He was wearing a derby ... I saw him. In Chernyshevsky Street.

ANDREI (*alarmed*): Where?

KAVALEROV: He was standing in the middle of the street. His derby had slid down on the back of his head. There he was, a short, fat man standing in the middle of the street, with his head thrown back. That's where Valya lives, on the second floor.

ANDREI: Did you see him there?

KAVALEROV: Uh-huh ... The pillow was in a yellow pillow case ... An old one ...

ANDREI: The rag picker ... standing under Valya's window.

KAVALEROV: Well, Valya's his daughter.

ANDREI: She's his adopted daughter. She's not his real daughter, she's just adopted. But that's all over now. She's left him. He doesn't have any rights at all over her. She's completely on her own. (*A pause.*) So he was standing under her window ...

KAVALEROV: Yes, he was.

ANDREI: Well, what about her? You didn't see her, did you? She didn't come to the window, did she?

KAVALEROV (*not answering right way*): No. Nobody came to the window. The only thing in the window was a little vase with a blue flower in it. (ANDREI *is silent.*) Why do you hate your brother so much?

ANDREI: He ought to be shot. (*At this point* ANDREI *sits down at his desk, begins working, becomes absorbed in it.* KAVALEROV *shaves.*)

KAVALEROV: I hate you, Andrei Petrovich. (*A pause.*) I hate you ... Are you listening? When you're working you don't hear a thing. What are you so absorbed in that you don't hear anything? (*A pause.*) Bureaucrat ... you stupid bureaucrat ... Now you're the master. You're one of the new aristocrats, Andrei Petrovich. I hate you. Because you're a man without imagination, a blockhead ... a sausage-maker. (*A pause.*) Why do you consider yourself a model child of the twentieth century, and me such a bad one? (*A pause.*) You're crushing me. Who gave you the right to crush me? How am I worse than you are? (*A pause.*) You're cleverer ... (*A pause.*) better organized ... (*A pause.*) stronger ... more important ... (*A pause.*) and that's why I have to acknowledge your superiority. You and I are going to have it out, my dear Andrei Petrovich. I'm 28 years old, and you're 40.

ANDREI (*jumps up again suddenly and explodes*): What?! What?! I beg your pardon? What's that you said? 40? Ha-ha-ha. (*He roars with laughter, he growls and snorts.*) 40 ... He said: 40 ... The nut ... you nut,

Kavalerov ... you joker ... 40 ... Listen ... you just said 40 ... no, not 40 ... We're going to sell it for 35 ... For 35 ... get it? There's close figuring for you ... Come over here ... (*Drags* KAVALEROV *to the desk, grabs the papers.*) Look ... I've figured it all out (*Loud laughter.*)

KAVALEROV: 40 ...

ANDREI (*bellows with laughter*): 35 ... It's terrific, it's stupendous ... It's a great triumph ... hurrah ... shout hurrah, Kavalerov. (KAVALEROV *is silent.*) Why are you looking at me that way?

KAVALEROV: I don't feel like shouting hurrah ...

ANDREI: You nut ... Why don't you? You don't believe that 70% veal salami can sell for 35 kopecks? Just take a look at this: Here's the complete set of figures. It's all perfectly clear.

KAVALEROV: It's all perfectly clear.

ANDREI: Then shout hurrah ... He doesn't say a word ... the joker.

KAVALEROV: All this salami business isn't getting us anywhere.

ANDREI: What do you mean, the salami business isn't getting us anywhere? You know, don't you, that every factory, industrial plant, and boarding school is going to buy our salami. (*They go look at the papers.*) Here's the analysis of its nutritive content. Take a look at those carbohydrates ...

KAVALEROV (*suddenly*): Bravo, bravo! All right, I'll shout hurrah. Hurrah, Andrei Petrovich, hurrah!

ANDREI: So you really do think it's terrific? If you ask me, it's terrific.

KAVALEROV: I can see that you're mighty pleased with yourself.

ANDREI: Well, of course. Why wouldn't I be, when it's such a success?

KAVALEROV: In this world great reputations are made because a new sort of sausage comes out of a machine. I look at you and I can see that the nature of glory has changed ...

ANDREI: If you ask me, it has changed. (VALYA *comes out from the terrace.*) So, you see, you did come, but I have to leave.

VALYA: I can come with you.

ANDREI: You can stay here awhile. Stay with Kavalerov.

KAVALEROV: Hello, Valya.

ANDREI: You know, Ivan's back?

VALYA: I know. Yesterday he came and stood under my window. He kept calling me.

ANDREI: And what'd you do?

VALYA: I hid and listened. He stood there for a whole hour. Then I couldn't help looking. I felt so sorry for him.

ANDREI: That was a mistake. You didn't have to look.

VALYA: But he kept calling me.

ANDREI: He can go to hell.

VALYA: That's cruel.

ANDREI: It isn't cruel. Not in the least. You don't have to worry about that.
VALYA: He's been reduced to groveling. He stood there for a whole hour.
ANDREI: Yes, he's reduced to groveling. Can you beat that ... so he stood under your window?
VALYA: For a whole hour.
ANDREI: It's all one of his little tricks. Don't believe anything he says. He likes to stand under windows. I know him. He even stands under my window.
VALYA: He was carrying a pillow. He said to me: Look, Valya, I've brought the pillow you used to sleep on.
ANDREI (*guffaws*): Really? What? The pillow you used to sleep on? Can you beat that ... But how's that pillow any worse than the one you're sleeping on now? Every pillow has its own story. So don't worry.
VALYA: You've seen him too, Kavalerov?
KAVALEROV: Yes, I've seen him.
ANDREI: Why didn't you tell me Valya'd been talking with him?
KAVALEROV: I'm not Valya's keeper.
ANDREI: You're two of a kind, Kavalerov. Right, Valya? They should get to know each other. Right, Valya? They'd have a lot in common ... Well, I'm going ... well, I'm going ... Are you coming with me? If not, stay here with Kavalerov. (*Suddenly.*) But what were you doing under Valya's window? (*To Valya.*) Stay here with him. He's been standing around under your window. (*After a pause, ironically.*) Doesn't he have a tragic face?
VALYA (*with a smile*): If you ask me, it's tragic. Why are you attacking Kavalerov? Kavalerov's a nice guy.
ANDREI: You think so?
VALYA: Yes, I think so ... (*A pause.*)
ANDREI (*looks at his watch*): Well, all right ... You know how much we'll sell the salami for? 35. Isn't that terrific? Well let's go. You coming? (*They go out through the glass door.*)
KAVALEROV (*calling after her, softly, leaving the rest unsaid*) Valya ... (*He holds the razor in his hands. He puts away his shaving equipment. The razor gleams in his hands. He confronts himself.*) Why did you kill Andrei Babichev? (*A Pause.*) Because you hated him. (*A Pause.*) No ... no. (*A Pause.*) Then why did you? (*A Pause.*) All my life, I've been in the background ... He took me in. He was my benefactor. Why did I raise my hand against him? (*A pause.*) Why did I kill Andrei Babichev?

(*Curtain.*)

Scene 2
"A Miracle Worker Appeared"

(*A kitchen. A stove, a faucet over a sink. Various entrances, hallways, flights of stairs. Several doors – of different heights. Street door above. A long stairway leads up to it. Morning. There are tenants in the kitchen.* LIZAVETA IVANOVNA, *a beautiful woman in an unfastened dressing gown. Small shelves, dishes, primus stove, steam.*)

FIRST TENANT (*at the stove, cooking. Something is boiling in a saucepan*): You shouldn't believe rumors. It's just stupid gossip.

SECOND TENANT (*polishing his shoes*): One of the guys I know at the office was telling me about it. He saw it all with his own eyes. There was this wedding. I even know where it took place: it was on Yakimanka Street. It was just an ordinary wedding. This tax collector was getting married. The guy from my office was there. And then all of a sudden this total stranger appeared at the wedding. He just walked right in – nobody knew who he was ... see? ... What a sight ... he was wearing a derby ... he didn't even take his derby off and he was carrying a pillow ... and I even know the details: it was a yellow pillow in a yellow pillow case.

FIRST TENANT: That's ridiculous. That's absolutely ridiculous.

SECOND TENANT: You think everything's ridiculous. But just listen ... and you listen, Lizaveta Ivanovna. You listen too. Amazing things are going on in Moscow.

LIZAVETA: But you'd better talk about it more quietly.

SECOND TENANT: Why should we keep quiet about it? It's not politics. Well then ... this total stranger in the derby carrying a yellow pillow showed up at the tax collector's wedding. He suddenly appeared and said (*Strikes a pose.*) "Why are you getting married? You shouldn't. You'll only be bringing your own worst enemies into the world!"

LIZAVETA: What business was it of his?

FIRST TENANT: It was incredible ... "Don't get married" – he said – "You shouldn't get married" ... "Our children are our own worst enemies." And listen to this: the bride fainted of course and the bridegroom was ready to start a fight. Then the stranger with the pillow left. The guests sat down at the table and began eating and having a good time. And suddenly, before their very eyes, all the wine in the bottles turned into water ... (*The door opens. The* THIRD TENANT *enters carrying a brief case – he's on his way to work.*)

SECOND TENANT (*repeats significantly*): All the wine turned into water ... (*Silence.*)

THIRD TENANT: What ... what? ... What are you talking about? About the man with the pillow? I've heard about it too ... they say that all sorts of things have been going on. A man with a pillow's walking around Moscow. He's going around looking for something ... in and out of apartments and beer joints ... honestly ... (*Silence.*)
FIRST TENANT: There's really nothing to it, my friends, nothing at all. People, at least the people on this street, want miracles to happen. Do you see what I mean? People lead dull lives. Understand? They want something unusual to happen ... But all this is just idle talk ... idle talk ... after all, look where we live. Are miracles really possible? ... Can wine really turn into water? (*A pause.*)
THIRD TENANT: God only knows ... maybe it's an advertisement ... Or maybe they're making a movie. But there are strange things going on here all right.
LIZAVETA (*to the* FIRST TENANT): Your milk will boil away ...
SECOND TENANT: It's true, we do lead dull lives. Boil the milk, clean up, go to work. But do you think a miracle worker really has appeared?
FIRST TENANT: What nonsense ...
THIRD TENANT: Why is it nonsense? Maybe he's not a real miracle worker, but some kind of hypnotist ... you know, mass suggestion ...
LIZAVETA: Just what's he suggesting? (*Silence.*)
SECOND TENANT: It's strange all right ... (*The* FIRST, SECOND *and* THIRD TENANTS *leave the kitchen.* LIZAVETA IVANOVNA *alone at the stove. A* YOUNG MAN *appears at the door at the top of the stairs.*)
YOUNG MAN (*with his elbows leaning on the railing, he looks down from the top of the stairs at* LIZAVETA IVANOVNA): You wouldn't go on sleeping with him unless you still loved him. How can you belong to me and stay married to him at the same time ...
LIZAVETA: Well, what do you want? Cut his throat if you like ... If I leave him, he'll kill both of us.
YOUNG MAN: Are you afraid?
LIZAVETA: Go ahead and cut his throat.
YOUNG MAN: Do you want me to cut his throat right now? (LIZAVETA IVANOVNA *is silent.*) Well, where is he? He hasn't gone out yet, has he?
LIZAVETA: I'm making him some hash.
YOUNG MAN: Aha, then he's still home. I can just picture it: he's sitting on the bed in his long underwear, scratching himself and thinking about what you'll bring him for breakfast. You slut, you, Liza ... (LIZAVETA IVANOVNA *is silent.*) You're a real slut.

You can love two men at the same time and sleep with them both. Either I'll slit his throat or he'll slit mine you don't care which. Why are you always coming out in the kitchen practically naked? I know why. You want everyone to get excited just looking at you. You're a whore. (*As he goes out, the* THIRD TENANT *leaves the door at the top of the stairs open. Blue sky is visible through the doorway. This is the exit to the yard. It's morning.* IVAN BABICHEV *appears in the doorway, a small, slovenly fat man in a derby. He's carrying by one corner a large dirty pillow in a yellow pillow case. He stops at the top of the stairs and listens.*)

LIZAVETA: I love you, you fool ...

YOUNG MAN: You're lying ... you love your husband just as much as you love me ...

LIZAVETA: There's the knife. (*She points to the knife lying on the stove. A pause.*) There's the knife ... (*The* YOUNG MAN *is silent.*) Coward ...

YOUNG MAN: All right ... (*He comes down the stairs to her.*) What are you smiling at ... You don't believe I'm capable of committing a crime for your sake?

A MAN'S VOICE FROM THE OTHER ROOM: Liza!

YOUNG MAN: Well go, your lord and master's calling ...

THE VOICE.: Liza!

LIZAVETA: Coward ...

YOUNG MAN: No, wait. No, I'm not a coward. But suppose I do cut his throat. So I go and slit his throat right now ... then they'll lock me up. I'll be behind bars for eight years, and what about you? You'll be living with other men ...

VOICE: Liza!

YOUNG MAN: Is that what you want? Listen. In just a minute you'll be gone and I'll be dead. I'll cut my own throat. Is that what you want?

LIZAVETA: That's just a lot of talk. (*She shouts to the other room.*) I'm coming! (*She goes out.*)

YOUNG MAN (*sits down on a small bench in a state of great agitation.*) What'll I do, what'll I do?

IVAN (*from above*): You should kill the husband.

YOUNG MAN (*jumps up*): What? Who's that? Who said that?

IVAN: If you want my opinion, you should slit the husband's throat ...

YOUNG MAN: What business is it of yours? You were eavesdropping!

IVAN: No need to get so angry, my friend. You see, I spend whole days, days and nights, walking about ... I go up and down other people's stairs. I look in other people's windows, I pick up other people's words. (*A pause.*) Why are you putting it off, young man? (*The knife*

gleams.) What are you waiting for? At this very moment the woman you love is kissing someone else ... listen how quiet it is in there. They're kissing.
YOUNG MAN: What a way to laugh. (IVAN *has come down into the kitchen. He sits down on a stool, takes off his derby, and puffs. He's put the pillow at his feet.*) Get the hell out of here, who are you anyhow? ... Maybe you came to steal the stove!
IVAN: I came in search of heroes.
YOUNG MAN: (*ironically*): Well, isn't that nice! So you heard our conversation.
IVAN: Yes, I did. And it gave me great pleasure. Really, aren't you going to act out this drama to the end? It had a great beginning.
YOUNG MAN: Listen, there's something really absurd about this. What would you like, for me to go all the way?
IVAN: I'm in search of heroes.
YOUNG MAN: Stop clowning. (*He looks him over carefully.*) A pillow ... I don't get it at all ... looks pretty suspicious to me ...
IVAN: You're a hero ... you're a real hero and you don't even suspect it. You ought to be proud of it ...
YOUNG MAN: I'll be late for work on account of you.
IVAN: I'm talking about jealousy.
YOUNG MAN (*angrily*): What?
IVAN: I mean your jealousy.
YOUNG MAN: That's none of your business.
IVAN: It is my business. You've got to kill that beautiful woman's husband. She's very beautiful. But you're right: she's a slut. You called her a slut ... in other words she's what was called in the old world a demonic woman.
YOUNG MAN: Really? ... Can you tell that right away? Good God, what'll I do?
IVAN: But you're not going to be intimidated ...
YOUNG MAN: What?
IVAN: What's holding you back? Jealousy is one of the grand old emotions ...
YOUNG MAN: What'll I do?
IVAN: Show your feelings. The old-fashioned feelings are beautiful. Love, hate, jealousy, pride, envy, pity ...
YOUNG MAN: You're quite an actor
IVAN: Young man, I'm a leader ...
YOUNG MAN: You're pulling my leg.
IVAN: I'm the leader of all those old-fashioned feelings. I'm the leader of a conspiracy and you're the standard-bearer of one of the great feelings – jealousy – you're an accomplice in my conspiracy.

YOUNG MAN: Oh really, what sort of rubbish is that! A guy walks into somebody else's house just like that ... (*A pause.*)
IVAN: Take the knife and go right in without knocking. She's in his arms at this very moment ...
YOUNG MAN: Tell me, do you really think she's beautiful? Were you struck by that right away?
IVAN: She sparkles like a glass vase, and right now your rival is pouring his love into that vase. Take the knife ...
YOUNG MAN: Oh, I can't ...
IVAN: Ssh ... listen ... a soft thud. That was the pillow falling. Their love-making knocked the pillow off the bed. Ssh. (*They stand at the door listening. Sudden commotion in the other room, then a frightful scream – the door flies open.* NEIGHBORS *appear. Anxious faces, uplifted hands, general panic. The* HUSBAND *appears at the door.*)
SECOND TENANT: What's the matter? What's happened?
HUSBAND: I'm all right. Just leave me alone, will you! You bastards! ...
FIRST TENANT: He's killed his wife! ...
FOURTH TENANT: He cut his wife's throat!!!
FIRST TENANT: Grab him!!!
HUSBAND: Get out of my way! ... Where is he? Where is he? Where is he? (*Goes up the stairs.*) Where's the lover-boy? (*He beats on the door where the* YOUNG MAN *went out.*) You bastard ... you bastard ... open the door ... or I'll break it down ... Open the door ... so you've been living with her? I'll kill you! I'll kill you! ...
A VOICE: Help!
ANOTHER VOICE: Police!
IVAN (*to the* YOUNG MAN *who is hiding behind* IVAN's *back*): What are you hiding for? No, no, come on out, young man, stop hiding. Come on out and answer for what you've done ... one always has to face the consequences of loving. (*He shouts to the* HUSBAND, *pointing to the* YOUNG MAN *hiding behind him.*) Here he is! Right here! ...
YOUNG MAN: A-a-a-ah! For God's sake, what are you doing? Don't let him ... save me ... a-a-a-ah ...
SECOND TENANT: The knife! ... he's seen the knife! ...
YOUNG MAN: A-a-a-a-ah ... (*The* HUSBAND, *seeing his rival, goes down the stairs. Silence.*)
FIRST TENANT: Grab him! ... (*The* HUSBAND *falls at* IVAN's *feet.*)
HUSBAND: I killed her ...
IVAN (*applauding*): Long live the good old human feelings! Long live jealousy! Long live love!
FIRST TENANT: He's a madman!
SECOND TENANT: Call the police!

IVAN: ...Where are you now, brother? Do you see now, brother Andrei! Follow me! ... all you cowards, jealous ones, lovers, heroes ... you knights in shining armor ... follow me ... the old world ... the old feelings – follow me ... I'll lead you on our last march.

(*Curtain.*)

Act II: Scene 3
"The Classical Repertory"

(ANDREI BABICHEV's *house. Evening.* ANDREI *at his work table.* IVAN.)

IVAN: We haven't seen each other for six months. How are all your state farms, and apiaries, and cafeterias? ...
ANDREI: I've invented a new kind of sausage, Vanya.
IVAN: And I've invented a machine.
ANDREI: Really? Good for you ... What kind of machine?
IVAN: Andrei, I've invented an amazing machine. You know: my greatest dream has always been the universal machine, the machine's machine. For years I've been thinking about the ideal instrument. My aim was to concentrate hundreds of different functions in one small apparatus ... I wanted to tame the mastodon of technology, harness it, and domesticate it ...
ANDREI: Good for you ... I envy you. You've got big ideas. It makes me feel ashamed of myself. Where will my salami get me? ... There you are with your mastodon of technology, while all I've got is some lousy old sausage ... Of course it does have 70% veal ... well, go on, go on.
IVAN: I've done it, Andrei. I've invented this machine ...
ANDREI (*suddenly*): Why do you drink so much, Vanya? You look pretty bloated.
IVAN: Don't interrupt me. I've invented a machine that can blow up mountains, that can fly, lift weights, crush stone. It's a perfect masterpiece of engineering. (*Suddenly.*) Why are you smiling?
ANDREI (*ironically*): From sheer pleasure. I'm anticipating what a great success you'll be. You'll be rendering an unforgettable service to your government. (*After a pause.*) Say: maybe it could even be of some use in making salami?
IVAN: It can do everything.
ANDREI: Well, I'll be damned ... we'll have to give you the Order of the Red Banner of Labor. What time is it? Eleven. It's late ... otherwise I'd

phone the patent office at the Commissariat of the National Economy in the Sovnarkom ...

IVAN: No point in doing that.

ANDREI: Why not?

IVAN: Wait a second, you didn't let me finish ... Once the machine was built I realized I had a miraculous opportunity to avenge my era. You won't get my machine – not you, or the patent office, or any part of this whole era of yours.

ANDREI: That's a great blow to us. Just think: we were getting so far behind and then you came along with your machine. You could have solved all our problems – in a flash your machine could have brought us into the golden age of technology.

IVAN: You're just making wisecracks, Andrei, while I'm being serious. Please stop making wisecracks. I repeat: I've invented an amazing machine. (*Silence.*) But you won't get it. I'm a knight in shining armor defending a dying era. I'm avenging my era – to which I'm indebted for the brains I've got in my head, brains that could devise such an amazing machine. Who'll get my machine? You? You devour us as though we were something to eat. You're swallowing the nineteenth century whole, the way a boa constrictor does a rabbit. You chew us, digest us, and then get rid of what you don't want. I don't want to be either digested or gotten rid of. You guzzle down our machinery and throw our feelings away ... I'll avenge our feelings. Do you know exactly what kind of machine I've invented?

ANDREI: No, Vanya, I don't know.

IVAN: While you're striving to turn man into a machine, I've already turned a machine into man. You're the new era, and I'm the old. And so I thumb my nose at you; in a burst of glory the dying century thumbs its nose at the one that's being born ... You won't get my machine! ...

ANDREI (*with a smirk*): You frighten me, Vanya.

IVAN: Do you understand what this means?

ANDREI: No, I don't understand.

IVAN: Even though it's the greatest creation of modern technology, I've endowed my machine with the pettiest of human feelings. I've corrupted the machine. I've turned the best machine in the world into a liar, and a cheap, sentimental scoundrel. At the celebration in Red Square for the October Revolution – I'll unveil it in front of everyone. You'll see, Andrei. It can blow up mountains, but I won't let it. Understand? I taught it to sing love songs, silly love songs from out of the past. It sings, gets sad, picks flowers, foolish flowers of the past. It falls in love, gets jealous, weeps, dreams, and that's not all ... Andrei,

you know what: it'll corrupt all your machines. That's how I've avenged my era ... which was a mother to me.
ANDREI (*softly*): You didn't invent anything, Vanya. That's an obsession of yours. You're not being very funny. What sort of a machine is this, anyway? Come on, now, could there really be such a machine?
IVAN: You don't believe it?
ANDREI: Sorry, I don't ...
IVAN: Watch out, Andrei ... this machine does exist. I named it Ophelia. That was the name of the girl who went mad from love ... I named my machine after the girl who went out of her mind from love and despair. Ophelia ... she drowned herself ...
ANDREI: Serves her right ... Now I'll tell you about my invention. You were talking about the machine's machine. Now imagine the salami's salami, the universal salami. Only I don't know what to name it – what about Ophelia, huh? Maybe name it Ophelia? Ophelia – that's the girl who went mad from love. Isn't there a girl in classical literature who ate too much salami? ...
IVAN: I hate you, Andrei. You're a graven image. You're a graven image with bulging eyes. You know what you look like? A piggy bank. I hate you, Andrei. (ANDREI *roars with laughter.*)
ANDREI: And just why do you hate me?
IVAN: You took my daughter away from me. (*Silence.*)
ANDREI: She left you of her own free will.
IVAN: Give me back my daughter ...
ANDREI: She's not your daughter. She's only adopted.
IVAN: I'm asking you, where's Valya?
ANDREI: She's living with a girl friend. You know that. You stood under her window. Don't act dumb. You kept calling her, but she wouldn't come back.
IVAN: Thanks to your planning, you told her what to do ...
ANDREI: You did everything you could to drive her out of her mind. If I hadn't done it, the police would have taken her away from you.
IVAN: You're a skunk.
ANDREI: Don't shout. If you're going to get nasty, I'll kick you right out the door.
IVAN: You skunk, you dirty old man ...
ANDREI: What?
IVAN: You're a dirty old man, you're corrupting Valya. (*Silence.*) How can you dare even dream of a girl like that, you salami maker? I'll strangle you with my bare hands. (*Silence.*) I know everything. Oh, you skunk. You want to breed a new race of people just the way you're breeding a new species of salami. You've selected my daughter.

My daughter's no incubator. Do you hear? My daughter's not going to be an incubator for you.

ANDREI: It's hard to make me angry. I'm a gentle soul. As the Director of the Food Trust, I deal with calves, lambs, fish, and bees. I've always been good natured, and nothing's going to change me now. Listen, Ivan, you say I'm a corrupter of youth. You've known for a long time that Valya's everything to me.

IVAN: Don't you dare talk about love. People of your era don't know what love is. You look at a woman as if she were a reservoir. Valya isn't going to be your reservoir. Do you hear? I'll kill you. (*Throws himself at* ANDREI, *who pushes him away,* IVAN *falls at his brother's feet. After a pause, at* ANDREI's *feet.*) Andryusha ... I'm sick ... I'm sick, Andryusha ...

ANDREI: You're not sick, Vanya. You're a son of a bitch, Vanya ...

IVAN: I'm miserable, Andryusha.

ANDREI: That's not true, Vanya. I don't feel sorry for you. You're just a phony. Vanya, they forgot to shoot you ... clear out of here ...

IVAN: So you're driving me away ...

ANDREI: Get going, Ivan Babichev ... I've got to work ... Clear out!

IVAN: All right, Andrei, I'm going, but just remember ...

ANDREI: Just remember what ... That's enough out of you ...

IVAN: Remember: You're talking to a leader ... you may be a leader, but I'm a leader too. Watch your step, Andrei ...

ANDREI: Okay, okay ...

IVAN: Don't go too far, Andrei ... I have a huge army behind me. I'm the leader of what you'd call the petty bourgeois. It's a peaceful conspiracy, a bloodless revolution of feelings ... it's a new kind of counter-revolution. (*He goes out.*)

ANDREI (*alone*): Too bad Kavalerov wasn't here. (*Walks back and forth, deep in thought. He goes over to the table, lifts the receiver off the phone, and begins speaking into it.*) 5-60-62. Yes. Uh-huh. Is this Comrade Shapiro? Hello, Solomon Davidovich. Yes, it's me. Hope I'm not calling too late. You're not asleep, yet? Listen Solomon Davidovich, how's my beauty? All locked up for the night, safe and sound? I'm in love with her. What? There's nothing dearer to me in the whole world. What? Uh-huh, uh-huh. When will I see her? Wednesday or Thursday? Give her my love. Uh-huh. I've been dreaming about her. So pink, so radiant, so tender. Uh-huh. You think we'll be able to sell her for 35 kopecks? But what'll we name her? You don't happen to know, do you, whether somewhere in the classics there's a girl who ate too much salami and went out of her mind from love? What? Uh-huh, uh-huh ... I'm just talking off the top of my head ... what? You mean nobody's going to be able to go out of their mind from love anymore?

What? ... A-a-h ... Uh-huh ... but in our new society there really won't be any such thing as going out of your mind from love? What? They won't be able to. Huh? What? So that's the way it's going to be? ... Well, okay. ... Good talking to you ... (*He puts the receiver down. Sits lost in thought. Takes the phone again and lifts the receiver.*) 5-60-62. Comrade Shapiro? You're not asleep yet? Tell me the truth. Is it all right if I get married? What? You're already asleep? Well, okay ... good night, then. (VALYA *enters.*) And here's another crazy female. You'll keep me from working. You can stay for ten minutes and that's it.

VALYA (*sits down on the sofa*): I'm awfully sleepy. Can I sleep on your sofa?

ANDREI: Kavalerov will be coming any minute now. He sleeps on the sofa.

VALYA: Kavalerov told me that when he first saw me passing by he felt as if a branch full of flowers and leaves had rustled past him. (ANDREI *is busy at his table, deeply engrossed in his work.*) Kavalerov says that you don't hear anything that's going on around you when you get engrossed in your work ... is that true? Andrei Babichev – fire! ... (*A pause.*) Kavalerov says you snore at night. There's a volcano called Krakatoa. You snore like that: Krra-Ka-Toa ...a ... Kraa ... Ka. ... To ... a ... It's revolting. (*A pause.*) Kavalerov says that you sing in the bathroom every morning. Very beautifully. (*Silence. It's not clear whether* ANDREI *hears her or not.*) I love you, Andrei Petrovich. I love you, dear Uncle Andrei, more than anything in the world. I promise you, dear, darling Uncle, undying love. I promise I'll be awfully good to you. I'm a very good-looking girl. I'm better than that salami you're always mooning over. Uncle ... do you hear me, Uncle? You're a glutton, a fat slob, do you hear what I'm saying to you? Look at me, idiot. (*Silence.*) We'll go to the football game together. I'll rustle in the wind like a branch full of flowers and leaves. But we won't take Kavalerov. Why did you take Kavalerov in anyway? I want to sleep on that sofa. I'm going to start getting undressed right now, I'll get undressed and go to bed. As soon as I'm all undressed you'll see what kind of a branch I am. It'll drive you mad. Uncle ... I'm starting to undress ... o-one-two-three ... the buttons have all popped open ... you don't even hear me, you miserable salami salesman. (*Silence. Sleepily.*) Let's go into the lab together. I'll show you some amazing things. You should study chemistry, Uncle. It'll help you in making packaged foods ... So long, Uncle, I'm falling asleep ... the bed springs are singing ... just listen to the springs singing ... little drops are trickling ... down from the vines of the sofa ... bunches of grapes ... I'm already asleep ... nite-nite ... nitwit ... (*Silence.* VALYA *sleeps.*)

ANDREI (*goes to the telephone, starts to lift the receiver, but thinks better of it and talks directly at the telephone*): It's me again. Yes, it's me, Solomon Davidovich. Wake up. I don't know what to do ... what should I do, Solomon Davidovich? She's here, she's sleeping on my sofa ... what should I do, Solomon Davidovich? Wake up, wake up, the President of the Board is talking to you ... what shall we name her? ... isn't there a girl in the classics who was in love with a salami salesman?

(*Curtain.*)

Scene 4
"I am a Beggar in this Frightful New World"

(ANDREI BABICHEV's *house. Early morning.* ANDREI *seated at the table.* SHAPIRO.)

SHAPIRO: I was just getting ready for bed. Five more minutes and I'd have been asleep. Then you phoned and said: "Shapiro, is it all right if I get married?" Then I got dressed again and came right over. This is a fine state of affairs. You've got me running around at all hours of the night.
ANDREI: I was thinking things over. Then I read for a while. Shakespeare's plays. See – it's one of Kavalerov's books.
SHAPIRO: And where is your Kavalerov?
ANDREI: I don't know. Maybe he's with that widow of his.
SHAPIRO: What widow?
ANDREI: It's a ghastly story. He got involved with an old bag in her forties when he was on a drunk. She's a cook, she fixes meals for the barbers' co-op. It's awful, you know, it's really tragic ... such grandiose expectations, and then suddenly he lands in an old bag's bed ... (*After a moment's silence.*) But I feel sorry for Kavalerov. What about hiring him to write jingles? Or have him write an opera about "The Quarter"?
SHAPIRO: I don't like the sound of any of this. What sort of behavior is that anyway, to pick up some drunk off the street and bring him home to live with you? That's straight out of Shakespeare.
ANDREI: And now I don't know what to do with him.
SHAPIRO: Tell him: "So long, take your Shakespeare and get out ..."
ANDREI: I just read *Othello* ... you know who Othello was, don't you?
SHAPIRO: Sure, everybody knows that. He was a Negro.

ANDREI: In the first place, he wasn't a Negro, he was a Moor, but that's not what's important. You know who he was – he was a general, governor-general of the island of Cyprus. The whole thing's really a military drama, a story of life in the barracks ... Iago is a line officer, Cassio is a desk officer ... and Desdemona is the sweetheart of the regiment ... and the whole thing's pretty great ... if you ask me, it's great ... General Othello was an ugly bastard. He was black and repulsive and everyone hated him. But he won the heart of Desdemona with tales of his great deeds in battle. She fell in love him because of all he'd been through. (*A Pause.*)

SHAPIRO: Aha ... I see, Kavalerov is beginning to have an influence on you. You're already starting to dream about heroes.

ANDREI: I had a brother named Roman. He threw a bomb at the governor. At the governor-general, who was a kind of Othello. They hanged him ...

SHAPIRO: Big deal ... just like in a novel, that's very romantic ... but it's harder to make a sausage. A bomb can be made any old way, but a sausage has to be nutritious.

ANDREI: You're right, Shapiro. I'm dreaming about heroes. I want salami-makers to be heroes, understand? But look at the kind of people I have to work with – all they want to do is take the line of least resistance. But I demand an enthusiastic approach. (*He gets carried away, stands up, and speaks as if to a large audience.*) You know what Prokudin did. He just came out with a cherry cordial candy and you know what he called it – "Rosa Luxemburg." How do you like that? I'm disgusted with Comrade Prokudin for taking the line of least resistance ... if Comrade Prokudin ever dreams up a new kind of piroshki, he'll probably call it "Lenin's Legacy" ... Words once written in blood Comrade Prokudin writes in sugar. That's taking the line of least resistance. Last week they put twelve new kinds of chocolates on the market. These are the names Comrade Prokudin had to offer: "Chanticleer," "Flight of the Bumblebee." And, if I remember correctly, "Odalisque." Comrade Prokudin proposes calling a Soviet candy "Odalisque." How do you like that? He's only got one line – "Rosa Luxemburg's" at one end, and "Odalisque's" at the other ... that's the line of least resistance. But anyhow, I've always said: names should come from the sciences. To make them sound intriguing. Some of the sciences are poetic – right, Shapiro? Like geography and astronomy. Use names like "Eskimo," "Telescope," "Equator" – Comrade Prokudin would never think of anything like that. I'm the one who ought to be thinking up names for candies. Even if I don't have the time, I've got to make it my business. Because, if I don't make it my business, I'll have horrible nightmares about Comrade

Prokudin putting a cake on the market called "The Last Flight of the Bumblebee." I've really got to look after everything myself. (*Pause.*) Yes, Shapiro, I demand an enthusiastic approach. Take this can, for instance ... (*He picks up a can from the table.*) Here's a can made by really enthusiastic workers. It's the product of one of our canneries in Vladivostok. What's in this can? Crab. Look at that blue. What a fine substantial can – bright and glorious as a ship's pennant. Enthusiastic workers made that can. (*Pause.*)

VALYA (*speaking from the bedroom*): Andrei Petrovich. (SHAPIRO *is utterly astonished.*) Andrei Petrovich ... Are you there? Uncle ...

SHAPIRO: Greetings! Andrei Petrovich isn't here. This is Shapiro. Andrei Petrovich went out in the garden to take a little walk. He took a volume of Shakespeare's plays with him and went into the garden. What are you doing in there?

VALYA: I sleep here. (ANDREI *keeps quiet and listens.*)

SHAPIRO: But do you have any right to sleep there? Are you already married?

VALYA: Not yet.

SHAPIRO: Are you in love with him?

VALYA: I have been ever since I was a child. It's awful ...

SHAPIRO: It's awful? ...

VALYA: That I'm in love.

SHAPIRO: You're an odd one! What's so awful about it ... on the contrary, it's great for a young girl to be in love.

VALYA: Who said that?

SHAPIRO: Shakespeare.

VALYA: Who?

SHAPIRO: Boris Shakespeare.

VALYA: His name's William ...

SHAPIRO: Oh yeah, I forgot ...

VALYA: It's disgraceful ...

SHAPIRO: What's disgraceful? That I forgot?

VALYA: That I'm in love . Love – that's a medieval emotion ...

SHAPIRO: Valya, you're pulling my leg ...

VALYA: There shouldn't be any such thing as love. Modern science will enable us to produce any feeling we want by artificial means. Just imagine the kind of machine there'd be. Your unhappy person comes along, say, somebody like Nikolai Kavalerov. He goes to the Institute of Emotions. That's the sort of institute there'll be: the "Institute of Emotions." So Kavalerov goes to the Institute of Emotions and announces: "I'm unhappy." Then a professor has Kavalerov sit down in front of the machine, puts the special head band on him – a chemically charged beam flashes back and forth – the machine starts to buzz-bzz-bzz-bzz ... it only takes a minute, and then, due to the action of that beam of light, William Kavalerov absorbs all the emotions you're supposed to feel in a perfect love affair. That's all there is to it ...

SHAPIRO: That's all very fine, my dear lady, but frankly, it bores me. Chemistry should be used chiefly for agricultural purposes ...

VALYA: You don't understand a thing. The new man must be absolutely rational. Andrei Petrovich doesn't understand anything either.

SHAPIRO: And all in all, Andrei Petrovich is a pretty awful person. Sure, he's a member of the All-Russian Central Executive Committee, he's been a party member for ten years – and then what does he go and do? He falls in love ...

VALYA: Do you think he really is in love?

SHAPIRO: Boy, is he! Like a knight in shining armor, a real feudal lord.

VALYA: Did he tell you he's in love?

SHAPIRO: No, he didn't. But it's a known fact that he went to the Institute of Emotions and declared: "I want to fall in love, put the head band on me." The professor had him sit down in front of the machine. The machine started to buzz-bzz-bzz-bzz – it only took a minute. Then Andrei Petrovich said: Thanks, now I'm all charged with emotions, I've fallen in love ...

VALYA: You're just kidding me ...

SHAPIRO: Of course I'm kidding. You know what Andrei Petrovich is – an elephant. If he went to the Institute of Emotions, and they told him that falling in love was forbidden, he'd smash all their equipment to pieces ...

ANDREI (*Suddenly*): That's enough ... it's beginning to bore me ...

SHAPIRO: Oh, you're here ...

VALYA (*looks out from the bedroom*): What's beginning to bore you?

ANDREI: Romance.

VALYA: You're just cross because I slept in your bed. And you didn't sleep all night. Where's Kavalerov?

ANDREI: He's been appointed Governor-General of the Island of Cyprus.

VALYA: Why are you so angry? I'm all dressed now. You can go to bed. (*Appears from the bedroom.*)

ANDREI: You don't say?

VALYA: What are you hissing at me for?

ANDREI: I didn't know I was hissing.

VALYA: Well, why don't you say: "Valya, I love you."

ANDREI: I won't be hissing if I say that ...

VALYA: Then add: "so much!" "Valya, I love you so much!"

ANDREI: Stop being so stupid. There's a little hissing for you.

SHAPIRO: It's beginning to bore me ...
ANDREI: What's beginning to bore you?
SHAPIRO: Romance. In the new world there won't be any such thing as love. Isn't that right, my dear lady? Modern science will enable us to produce any feelings we want by artificial means. There'll be an "Institute of Emotions."
ANDREI: Who said so?
SHAPIRO: Shakespeare.
ANDREI: Your Shakespeare's an idiot.
KAVALEROV (*comes in from the terrace. To* VALYA): You're here, Valya? What are you doing here? Did you spend the night here?
SHAPIRO: What business is it of yours, Comrade Kavalerov? What difference does it make where Valya spent the night?
KAVALEROV: Andrei Petrovich, I think I'll be moving out now ... for good ... and I want you to listen to what I've got to say ...
ANDREI: Go ahead.
KAVALEROV: I want to talk about Valya.
ANDREI: Valya, he wants to talk about you.
KAVALEROV: Can I say whatever I want?
ANDREI: Go ahead.
KAVALEROV: It's not possible for a young girl to really be in love with a forty-year-old man. It's just your position that impresses her. She isn't in love with you. I've been doing a lot of thinking ... I've thought over carefully what I'm going to say ... (*Pause.*) I don't have the right to tell you what to do. But it seems to me you're on the verge of doing something that a good Communist wouldn't do ...
ANDREI: All right.
KAVALEROV: I don't want to make you angry. I'm talking to you man to man. Fate brought us together in a strange way. I can see that you and I are going to come into conflict. Because of the difference in our positions in life, and Valya.
VALYA: And what?
KAVALEROV: And you, Valya.
VALYA (*to* ANDREI): What did he say?
KAVALEROV: I love you, Valya. I mean that from the bottom of my heart. Tell me ...
VALYA: What's he talking about ... What am I supposed to say?
KAVALEROV: Valya, why don't you tell me the truth ... You spent the night here because you ... because you're already married?
VALYA: Leave me alone ... (*Silence.*)
KAVALEROV: Then that means ... it means that ... You've taken everything I have away from me, Andrei Petrovich ... all my dreams of life and love ...

ANDREI: I haven't taken anything away from you, Kavalerov.
KAVALEROV: Can't you see how unfairly I've been treated? I don't have anything to live for. It's perfectly clear. Everything belongs to you. And I'm just a beggar in this terrifying new world. Give Valya back to me, Andrei Petrovich. (*Silence.*) Give Valya back to me. You don't need her. You've already reached the top.
ANDREI: You're talking very strangely, Kavalerov. Valya, I don't get it at all. Help us, Shapiro.
KAVALEROV: Don't you dare bring Shapiro into this. (*To* SHAPIRO.) Get out of here. You pimp! Valya, why don't you say something?
VALYA: I don't have anything to say. I think you're drunk. It'd be better if you left ...
KAVALEROV: I don't have anywhere to go. Where could I go? Back to being a bum? But you ... you'll stay here ... to perform your function ...
VALYA: What function?
KAVALEROV: You know what function ... being a reservoir ...
SHAPIRO: He's crazy ...
VALYA: I don't know what's going on, Uncle ...
KAVALEROV: But maybe you'll come to me later on ... in a month or so, and let me have the reservoir that others have already made use of.
ANDREI: What did you say? Reservoir? ... Oh, I get it. Those are the very words my brother Ivan used. Then that means you've already met Ivan? I'm very glad. Congratulations, Kavalerov.
KAVALEROV: Yes! I'm prepared to defend your brother and his daughter. I'll fight for him and his daughter against you. You've cheated her out of tenderness, genuine feeling, individuality, and everything else you try to suppress. Don't believe him, Valya. You're just something for him to play around with. (*Suddenly notices how threatening* ANDREI's *silence is becoming.*) No ... no ... wait ... don't get angry ... Really ... I'm only joking ... I'm drunk. Honestly ... I'm completely drunk. Why don't you say something? ... Well, don't if you don't want to. Really, Comrade, it's all a misunderstanding ... absolute nonsense ... (*A pause.*) I'm all on edge ... I'm exhausted ... I'm in a state of nervous collapse. I ought to take cold showers ... I'll do calisthenics with you. Will you let me? ... All right? ... We could, couldn't we? Why don't you say something, Andrei Petrovich? Valya, tell him ... Well, all right, so you don't want to talk to me, what do you want me to do, then? (IVAN *looks in the window from the terrace.*) Go away, right? Just like a dog. But where? To the Widow Prokopovich? To some old bag's bed. And Valya will stay here. That means I'll never see Valya again. To go away ... (*Silence.*) How can I just go away after what's happened? Something's got to be done about this. I insulted you – so

why don't you hit me? (*Silence.*) Or maybe you and I don't speak the same language? Yes, of course, that's it. You're a Communist, you're busy building a new way of life, but I'm just a poor intellectual. I challenge you to a duel, do you hear? (*Silence.*) You've got weapons here. We'll fight. Give me a revolver. I'm not going to just leave. Do you hear, I won't leave. (*Silence.*) I'm insulting you, so you'll have to fight. Do you hear? ... You sausage-maker ... sausage-maker ... seducing a young girl like that ... you child-raper. (*Up until this point* VALYA *has maintained an embarrassed silence.*)

VALYA (*to* ANDREI): Why don't you say something?
ANDREI: It's a temporary fit of insanity. What can I do?
VALYA: I'm leaving. (*Goes quickly to the door to the terrace.*)
ANDREI: Valya ... (VALYA *comes back and slaps* KAVALEROV *in the face.*)
SHAPIRO: Serves him right!
KAVALEROV: All right ... I'll go ... what in the ... Where are my things? (*Looks everywhere, picks up a book from the table.*) This is my book ... yes ... here's my razor ... (*Picks up the razor.*) It's mine all right ... (*Sees* IVAN *in the window.*)
IVAN (*whipping the derby off his head*): Greetings, Andryusha. You know what this is called? It's called the sexual counter-revolution. Come here, Kavalerov. Oh, my poor friend! Come here. Oh, you'll certainly be the leading man in my company. (KAVALEROV *goes out on the terrace and can be seen leaning on* IVAN's *shoulder.*) Andryusha, did you notice, he took his razor with him? ...

(*Curtain.*)

Act III: Scene 5
"Youth Has Passed"

(*At* ANNICHKA PROKOPOVICH's *house. A small, ugly, musty room crowded with so much furniture it's hard to move about. The room is dominated by a huge bed. It casts a towering shadow like a temple. It is evening.* IVAN, ANNICHKA, KAVALEROV.)

IVAN: So this is it, is it? Um-hmm ... so this is the place where Kavalerov's been living. You know, Anna Mikhailovna, your room's already becoming a part of history. "Nikolai Kavalerov lived here." And you're becoming part of history too, Anna Mikhailovna. After all, you're the – wife, or at least the girl friend of Nikolai Kavalerov.

KAVALEROV: What are you making such a face for, Ivan Petrovich?
ANNICHKA: Kolya hates me.
IVAN: Kavalerov, it's not right, to hate such a nice lady. After all, Anna Mikhailovna let you climb into her remarkable bed. Just look at it, rosewood, mirrored arches, cupids dancing, apples rolling out of horns of plenty ...
ANNICHKA: My late husband won this bed in the lottery ...
IVAN: There, you see. It's a family heirloom. But you despise her. You were offered love, a family, an heirloom, a legend in the making – but you refused. And then there's Anna Mikhailovna herself. Take a good look at her: how expansive she is, how soft, how kind. Anna Mikhailovna, didn't you ever dream you turned into a bed? I'm amazed at you, Kavalerov. Nice people like Anna Mikhailovna and my brother Andrei take you into their homes ... and yet you behave so obnoxiously everywhere you go ... and you hate absolutely everyone ... (KAVALEROV *remains silent*.)
ANNICHKA: A new movie theatre just opened next door. It's a great theatre. It's called the Fantasma. It's right around the corner. We could all go to a movie.
IVAN: Sure we could! That's a wonderful idea!!! You know, Kavalerov, we've been talking a lot about feelings ... but we've forgotten the most important one of all: indifference ... of course ... I consider indifference the highest state the human mind can attain. Let's be indifferent, Kavalerov. Look: we've discovered true peace. (*Points to* ANNICHKA, *then the bed.*) Kavalerov, we ought to drink to indifference and to Annichka. (*Silence.*) Women were once the shining light of our civilization, the symbol of all that was pure and beautiful. I was searching for the essence of womanhood ... but Valya left me for him. I thought a woman was something that belonged to you, and that her tenderness and love was only meant for you, but that's where I was wrong ... Valya left me for him. After something like that, is anything worth fighting for? Isn't it time to stop caring, Kavalerov? After all, she really does love him. Nobody actually stole her. She ran out on you.
KAVALEROV: I'll get Valya away from him.
IVAN: Oh, no, Kavalerov ... no, you won't get her away from him ... she won't leave him for you. Your youth is over, Kavalerov.
KAVALEROV: That's not true. I'm 28. He's older than I am, and she doesn't love him.
IVAN: You're a thousand years old, Kavalerov. Stop giggling, Anna Mikhailovna. He's old, your friend Kolya – he's ancient ... he's weighed down with all the old age of our epoch and suffers from all the rheumatism. But that brother of mine – he's young and energetic,

he's on top of the world. He's got his nose stuck so high in the air he doesn't even see us. Look, Kavalerov, there's your destiny – a bed, a warm comforter, a warm Anna Mikhailovna ... what else do you have to look forward to? Look what you've turned out to be ... a clown, a little boy who never grew up. I know that's hard to take, it's sad ... yes, I know, there's Chernyshevsky Street somewhere out there ... open windows on the second floor, clouds float across the sky, and their paths merge with their reflections in the window panes. And a girl was leaning on the window sill, her arm delicate as a flute. You'd better forget about all that, that's not for you with your big red nose ... your youth is over ... you're not going to be handsome or famous. You won't be coming from a small town to the capital, you won't be a general or a scholar or a long-distance runner or an adventurer ... it's all over for you ... you're old enough to be a father yourself. You ought to have a son of your own.

ANNICHKA: There, you see, Kolya. Ivan Petrovich is saying just what I've been saying all along. That's what I've been telling you: you'll settle down when we have a baby.

IVAN: Then what's the matter? You're a fascinating woman, Anna Mikhailovna. Take him to your bosom. Rock the tired old century to sleep in your arms. Hurrah! ... Bear him a child, Anna Mikhailovna. We'll put it on this little pillow of mine. We'll celebrate the birth of a true child of the October Revolution ... if it's a boy, we'll call him "The Quarter," if it's a girl, we'll call her "Ophelia." Let's drink, Kavalerov, let's drink to youth which has passed, and to the conspiracy of feelings which has failed.

KAVALEROV: You're a son of a bitch, Ivan Petrovich. My youth isn't over. No ... (*Grabs* IVAN *by the collar.*) It's not true, do you hear? I'll prove it to you ... do you hear?

ANNICHKA: Don't shout, Kolya ... don't make a scene ...

KAVALEROV: Shut up ... get back to your kitchen ... I'm not in the same class with you, you pig ... do you hear?! ... you got me in your clutches when I was drunk ... it was all a big mistake, understand ...

ANNICHKA: But you kissed me so passionately that night ... you said: "Annichka, it's so wonderful, after all those prostitutes, to hold a pure woman in my arms" ...

KAVALEROV: This is awful ... this is awful! ... of course she's nothing but a dumb broad, but you, Ivan Petrovich, why are you making fun of me? Well, why don't you tell her, tell her ... tell her her face looks like a rusty padlock ... tell her she's an old bag coming apart at the seams, you can squeeze her out like liver paste ... (*After a pause, exhausted.*) Let me alone ... Go away. Get out. (*A pause. He staggers from exhaustion.*) What should I do, Ivan Petrovich, what should I do?

IVAN: Kill my brother Andrei. (*Silence.*)
KAVALEROV: You're the one ... you're the one that ought to be killed for stirring up all this trouble. (*Silence.*)
ANNICHKA: God knows what you're talking about ...
IVAN: You wanted fame. This will make you famous. Your name will be honored by posterity as the hired assassin who murdered the century. I give you my blessing.
KAVALEROV: Get out. Leave me alone. (*He drags himself towards the bed. Falls on the bed. Silence.*)
IVAN: Well, how about it, Anna Mikhailovna, shall we go to the Fantasma? Let's let Kavalerov sleep.
ANNICHKA: It's right around the corner. You don't even have to put a hat on. I'll just take a scarf.
KAVALEROV (*raising himself up*): I don't know why, Ivan Petrovich, but I have a feeling ... that Valya is going to come here ... really I do ... tell her how to get here ... it's easy to get lost in the corridors here. Maybe she'll come to make up for being so cruel to me.
IVAN: You're making Anna Mikhailovna jealous for nothing by talking that way ... Don't get upset, Anna Mikhailovna, nobody's going to come to him. Oh, you look just like Carmen in that scarf! I'd carry you over my head like a torch, but alas ... you're not a torch at all, but a whole searchlight ... (*They all go out.*)
(KAVALEROV *lies on the bed. Everything is quiet. Here* KAVALEROV's *dream begins. The stage seems to vibrate. All at once the shadows shift position as if an invisible source of light had sprung up somewhere from within the depths of the furniture – an unpleasant yellowish light. A knock at the door.* KAVALEROV *sits up on the bed.*)
KAVALEROV: Come in! ... (VALYA *enters. She seems to float in, the essence of femininity, tender, touching.* KAVALEROV *sits on the bed.*) There ... I knew it ... I've been waiting. (ANDREI BABICHEV *enters.* KAVALEROV *recoils.* ANDREI *and* VALYA *sit down at the table. They don't see* KAVALEROV. *He's in plain sight, but they don't see him – it's a dream.*)
ANDREI: Ah-ha ... say, this is great ... if you ask me, it's great ...
KAVALEROV (*from the bed*): Hello, Andrei Petrovich ...
ANDREI: This is where we'll have the wedding. If you ask me, it's a great place.
KAVALEROV: Valya, here I am ...
VALYA (*without seeing or hearing him*): Why'd you bring me here?
ANDREI: Why, don't you like it here? Look, that's quite a bed, made out of rosewood ...
KAVALEROV (*seized with fear*): Andrei Petrovich ...
ANDREI (*without seeing or hearing him*): Are you embarrassed? ... are you ashamed? ...

VALYA: I don't know ... (ANDREI *laughs loudly. In the dream* ANDREI *looks the way he appears in* KAVALEROV's *imagination, he's frighteningly inhuman like a statue or a scarecrow.*)
KAVALEROV: You're not alone, Andrei Petrovich. I'm here – Kavalerov! Can't you see me? Here I am!
ANDREI: I'll undress you now ...
KAVALEROV (*screams*): Valya!
ANDREI: What are you sighing for? ...
VALYA: Someone's calling me ...
KAVALEROV: Valya, here I am! ...
ANDREI: Who's calling you? What nonsense. That's mysticism. That's a lot of mysticism. It's all very simple. Now we're going to go to bed together. What's the point of mysticism?
KAVALEROV (*screams, but without being seen or heard*): I won't let you ... do you hear ... the bastards ... why doesn't he hear me?
VALYA: I feel so sad.
ANDREI: You little fool ... Ivan taught you that ... what do you want anyhow? For me to start sighing? ...
VALYA: I want to see Kavalerov.
KAVALEROV: Valya, Valya ... look ... I'm over here ... look, here I am ... what's going on here ... I'm screaming, "Valya, Valya" as loud as I can ... can't you see me ... here I am, see, here are my hands. Here I am, I'm standing right next to you ... Valya ... My God ... she doesn't see me ...
VALYA: I want to see Kavalerov.
ANDREI: I'll have him put away in a lunatic asylum ...
VALYA: You're a tyrant.
KAVALEROV: Quit trying to kid me, Andrei Petrovich. You're just pretending not to see me. Don't be afraid, Valya, don't be afraid. Look at me, I'm right here next to you, I'll save you, I've been waiting for you all my life ... Valya ... Valya ... they want to marry me off to Annichka ... Valya take pity on me ... (*Gets down on his knees before her, throws his arms around her legs.*) Take pity on me ... I'm right here ... you don't see me, you don't feel my hands, even though I'm touching your knees ...
VALYA (*without seeing or hearing him*): Kavalerov saw me at the recreation center. I was in my shorts. He said my knees were sweet as oranges. You never say things like that to me.
ANDREI: Corpses talk like that. That's the language of the dead.
KAVALEROV: I'm not dead.
ANDREI: You're a reservoir, Valya ... do you understand? You're an incubator ... We'll sleep together in that big comfortable bed and then you'll have a baby. We've got to have descendants. All the rest is mysticism ...

KAVALEROV: Don't sleep with him, Valya ... don't waste your youth on him: you hear what he's saying, don't you? He's saying you're a reservoir. Valya, he's an insensitive boor, he's a monster ... he's a machine ...
VALYA: I won't go to bed with you! ...
ANDREI: Oh yes you will! ...
VALYA: I'll scream! ... Kavalerov! ...
KAVALEROV: I'm right here! ...
VALYA: Kavalerov! ...
KAVALEROV: I'm right here! ...
VALYA: Kavalerov! ...
KAVALEROV: Here I am ... here I am ... I'm right over here. Over here ...
VALYA: Save me, Kavalerov! ...
KAVALEROV: What'll I do? ... he doesn't even see me. (*There's a bottle on the table,* KAVALEROV *grabs it. He can't lift it. It's a dream. The bottle seems glued to the table.*) Ah-ah-ah-ah-ah ...
ANDREI: Stop screaming ... you can forget the word "love." That's an obsolete concept. What are you afraid of? There'll be one gigantic apartment building with rows of mass production bedrooms ... 20,000 sex acts per day. But what do you want? ... individual portions ... sweet little kisses ... caresses ... sighs. To hell with all that! That's the old-fashioned home-made way ... I'll kick the stuffing out of all those little kisses ... Throw them out! ... I'll build the perfect mass production bedroom. Pretty great, huh?
VALYA: You make me feel trapped! Let me go to Kavalerov. He said that I rushed past him like a branch full of flowers and leaves ... Kavalerov, where are you? ...
KAVALEROV: I'm right here ...
VALYA (*speaks without seeing or hearing* KAVALEROV): Where are you? You won't have to live in back alleys anymore. I want to be with you ...
ANDREI: Be quiet ...
VALYA: It's me! It's me! The one you've been waiting for all your life. Here's my hand, delicate as a flute ... Your youth hasn't passed. No ... I love you ... I'll save you ... dearest ... darling ... where are you? ...
KAVALEROV: I'm right here ...
ANDREI (*as if he suddenly just caught sight of* KAVALEROV. *In a terrible rage*): Doctor!!! (*A* DOCTOR *appears wearing a white uniform. Black beard. Glasses. Yellow bald spot. Bony.*)
KAVALEROV (*cries out in terror, like someone having a nightmare*): Don't! Don't! Don't!

DOCTOR (*in a jerky voice, as if he wasn't able to talk, but had been taught how*): Where's the patient?
ANDREI: There's the patient.
DOCTOR: Ahah ... (*Squealing with delight.*)
KAVALEROV: Valya ...
DOCTOR: Take off his jacket. Give me a hand ... that's it ... (ANDREI *helps the* DOCTOR *undress* KAVALEROV.) Let's just take off his shirt now ...
KAVALEROV: I don't want to. I'm ashamed ... Valya, I'm ashamed, don't, don't ...
ANDREI: Just take it off ... that's it ... quite a handsome guy ... (*They undress* KAVALEROV, *who looks pathetic.*)
DOCTOR: Uh huh ... uh huh ... just a minute ... let's have a look at the muscles ... uh huh ... quite a flabby set of muscles ... uh huh ... loose living, must come from loose living ... well now, just step over here to the light ... come over to the light now ... Let me take a look at your pupils ... let's see those pupils ... let's take a look at them ... let's see how they respond ... just step over here to the light ... (*He pulls* KAVALEROV.) Uh huh ... uh huh, uh huh ... just a little nearer to the light ... yessir ... uh uh uh uh ... (*Shouts, his voice going higher and higher.*) He's stark – raving – mad! ... (*They all rush over to* KAVALEROV.)
KAVALEROV: Forgive me ... forgive me ... (*He falls on the bed. He wakes up.* KAVALEROV's *dream comes to an end. The stage once again assumes its former appearance.* ANNA PROKOPOVICH *enters on tip toe.*) Let me go ... let me go ... I'm coming! ... I'll save her ... let me go ... (*He screams.*) Valya! Valya! ... (*He continues to scream as the curtain falls.*)

(*Curtain.*)

Act IV: Scene 6
"Name Day Party"

(*A small room. Petty bourgeois. The* LADY OF THE HOUSE *is celebrating her name day. A table laden with sumptuous fare. A hanging lamp with a very broad orange lamp shade. The group applauds as* IVAN BABICHEV *and* NIKOLAI KAVALEROV *enter, led in by the master of ceremonies,* MIKHAIL MIKHAILYCH. IVAN *is carrying his pillow.* NIKOLAI KAVALEROV *looks like a sleepwalker. His reddish hair is unkempt.*)

MIKHAIL MIKHAILYCH: Ladies and gentlemen, may I have your attention for just a moment, please? ... Quiet, please ... ssh ... With your permission, ladies and gentlemen, today, for Elena Pavlovna's name day, I've decided to ... it's a kind of a present ... and for her gift, here's what I've arranged: I've invited the famous man we've all been hearing so much about. The man I've invited to be here with us tonight is none other than (*Points with a sweeping gesture.*) Ivan Petrovich Babichev! ... I just ran into him on the street. Ivan Petrovich has been stirring people up to rise in revolt against his brother.

LADY IN GREEN: But who is his brother?

MIKHAIL MIKHAILYCH: Now please don't interrupt, ladies and gentlemen. Before we do anything else, we should all give Ivan Petrovich a rousing welcome. If I may be allowed to express myself this way, Ivan Babichev is the great prophet of the twentieth century ...

GUESTS: Bravo ... bravo ... bravo!

IVAN: Greetings, my friends, greetings ... Congratulations, Elena Pavlovna, let's wish her many happy returns, my friends ...

VENERABLE OLD MAN: Please sit down and make yourself at home ...

IVAN: And here's Nikolai Kavalerov, a man of humble origin and grandiose ideas ... sit down, Nikolai Kavalerov ...

KAVALEROV: All right, I'll sit down, it's all the same to me: you can do whatever you want.

LADY OF THE HOUSE: Very pleased to meet you ... make yourself at home. May I pour you some wine?

IVAN: Thank you. (*A pause.*) Can you all see me all right? Move back just a little, would you please ... I want you all to see me.

OLD MAN: Bravo ....

MIKHAIL MIKHAILYCH: Quiet ... ssh ... it's about to begin. (*Tension begins to mount in the* CROWD.)

IVAN (*raises his wine glass*): I drink to your health, my friends ... (*A pause.*) Everyone look at me. I'm your king. Take a good look at me. (*A pause.*)

KAVALEROV (*maliciously*): Oh no, he's not crazy. You think he's crazy? He's a crook ...

A VERY DRUNK GUEST: Right! (*A pause.*)

IVAN: I'm your king. Take a good look at me! I'm a fat guy. I've got a bald spot. The bags under my eyes hang down like violet stockings. Look at me! Remember this moment well! This is Ivan Babichev you're looking at. When they ask you "What did Ivan Babichev look like?" then you'll be able to tell them about me ... See this derby. My derby's rusty-brown with age. My derby's begun to look like an Easter cake. (*A pause.*) Look at me. A king sits before you. I am the king of the cheap, the shabby, and the vulgar ...

VIC (*enthusiastic young man, asks in amazement*): But what's the pillow for?

IVAN: It's my coat-of-arms. It's your coat-of-arms, my dear people. It's an old pillow, honored by the many heads that have slept on it.

OLD MAN: Bravo, bravo ...

IVAN: See, I'm putting it down at my feet. And it just sat down there like a pig.

VERY DRUNK GUEST: Right ...

ZINOCHKA (*in the hush that follows*): Tell me: is it true that you know how to perform miracles?

IVAN (*in the ensuing silence*): Yes, it's true ... (*A pause.*)

LADY OF THE HOUSE: Mikhail Mikhailych, ask your friend to perform a miracle ...

KAVALEROV: Show them a miracle, Ivan Petrovich. (*Throughout what follows* KAVALEROV *puts his head down on the table and remains indifferent to what's going on around him, as if asleep.*)

IVAN: All right, my friends, I agree ...

OLD MAN: Wonderful ... wonderful ...

MIKHAIL MIKHAILYCH: Comrade Babichev is a twentieth-century miracle worker.

IVAN: I agree to perform a miracle, but first, each of you has got to confess his innermost desires.

VERY DRUNK GUEST: Right. (*A hush falls over the group.*)

LADY IN GREEN: But people's innermost desires are often indecent. (*A pause.*) What do we do in that case?

LESS VENERABLE OLD MAN: That's not so easy – to confess your innermost desires.

IVAN: I'm waiting. Who'll be the first? (*Laughing and giggling, they crowd around* IVAN.)

ZINOCHKA: Well, I'd like to ... (*She stops short.*) Oh, no!

MIKHAIL MIKHAILYCH: Don't be embarrassed, Zinaida Mikhailovna. This is beginning to get interesting.

ZINOCHKA: Let somebody else start. (*A pause.*)

MIKHAIL MIKHAILYCH: Then let me. This is a deeply personal matter, and it'll probably seem funny to everyone else, but, with your permission, I'll go ahead and tell you about it anyhow. My wife's eight months pregnant ... you see, my greatest desire is a small one, really, but it's very important to me ... a father's fondest hope, so to speak ... would it be possible for the baby to look like me?

IVAN: Bravo, bravo! ...

OLD MAN: Well, all right ... then I'll be next ... it's not so bad after all. Well, my wish is just a simple human one ... a desire for peace and quiet ... well, that's it. I'm sixty years old. I'd like to own my own house. Just a little house, a bungalow in the country. With a garden and a flowering hedge – and jasmine blooming. And a verandah opening out on the garden ... braided rugs, a piano with a silk cover, an awning that rolls down from the window. Peace, quiet ... On Sundays the whole family comes to visit me: my old brother, my uncle who's a hundred, my sons the engineers, and all the grandchildren ... We all sit on the verandah and eat raspberries. My granddaughter plays a serenade by Drigo on the piano. We eat raspberries. And the youngest one crawls on the grass with raspberry all over his face ...

LADY OF THE HOUSE: Ah, how lovely ...

OLD MAN: A big family. A quiet house. Patches of sunlight on the floor. Where is all that? Why doesn't my granddaughter play the piano? I'm an old man, I need a quiet little house.

LADY OF THE HOUSE: Ah, how lovely ... (*Silence.*)

VIC (*all of a sudden, impetuously*): But I'd like ... but I'd like ... wait ... I dream about having an extraordinary love affair ...

LESS DRUNK GUEST: Oh, you devil ...

VIC (*passionately*): I dream about having an extraordinary love affair ... do you suppose I could? That's what I wanted to say ... I'm an electrical engineer by profession ... I often have to go into other people's apartments. And what do I see there? Fights, perpetual bickering. Hate, screaming at children ... it shouldn't be that way ... our hearts should be overflowing with happiness.

VERY DRUNK GUEST: Right.

VIC: So what I want to say is: my secret wish is to love a woman with an undying passion.

IVAN: Bravo ...

LADY OF THE HOUSE: Well, now it's my turn ... you see, there's my daughter Zina.

ZINOCHKA: Oh, Mama don't ...

LADY OF THE HOUSE: Just a minute, Zinochka. Don't interrupt ... if this man can help us, why not tell him all about it? Here's my Zinochka ... she's very talented ...

ZINOCHKA: Oh, Mama, how can you ...

LADY OF THE HOUSE: She sings beautifully ... and I'd like ... it would be so easy to make my dreams come true. Of course, I'm a mother, and I want my daughter to have everything in life. I'm so anxious for Zinochka to be famous throughout the whole world. That's really not so far-fetched. She has a voice like an angel. Is it really so sinful to want wealth and fame for your child?

LESS VENERABLE OLD MAN (*with sudden vehemence, in a threatening tone*): Tell me now, why are you eating your heart out? Why do you hate your next-door neighbor? On account of a room?

OLD MAN (*excitedly*): What's that?

LESS VENERABLE GUEST: Let's say that I'm here. And let's say that you're there – Sergei Nikolaevich, Mr. Mikulitsky ... That makes us neighbors then, we live right next door to each other.

OLD MAN: Well, what of it?

LESS VENERABLE OLD MAN: And let's say I know that you're a venerable old man, an old man that everybody respects. But I just happen to live right next door to you, with only a thin wall between us, and I listen every night to hear if you're dying yet. So every morning I get up and start swearing because the old man hasn't died yet. He's still alive and kicking even though he's got one foot in the grave. Here's my wish: If you asked: "What's your secret desire" – I'd tell you: "I wish you'd die, neighbor, I wish you'd die, Sergei Nikolaevich Mikulitsky!" That's my wish. So your room would be empty.

VIC: That's disgraceful ...

OLD MAN: For god's sake, Elena Pavlovna, why do you let him! (*The* OLD MAN *sobs. General indignation.*)

ELENA PAVLOVNA: It's a disgrace ... it's a disgrace ... aren't you ashamed, Nikitin ...

LESS VENERABLE OLD MAN: Of course, I apologize ... I'm awfully ashamed of myself.

OLD MAN: Just how low can a person sink?

LESS VENERABLE OLD MAN: It's shameful but true.

IVAN: So now I've heard you all ... everything's just fine. I've listened carefully to everything. All that remains to be done now is to fulfill your wishes.

VIC: Our lives are boring, our lives are worthless. Nothing but sadness. Hatred and fighting ...

LADY IN GREEN: You mean you can make our wishes come true?

IVAN: I can't make your wishes come true. I'm the king of the dead.

LADY IN GREEN: In other words, you've tricked us?

IVAN: Dead men don't have desires. I'm the king of corpses.

ZINOCHKA (*passionately*): That's not true. I'm going to be a famous singer.

IVAN: My dear girl, they won't let you be famous.

LADY OF THE HOUSE: Who won't?

IVAN: My brother, Andrei Babichev. (*Silence.*) My brother, Andrei Babichev, builder of the new world, will destroy vanity, love, the family, cruelty ...
OLD MAN: What does all that mean?
IVAN: You were talking about family, my dear sir – there won't be families anymore. You wished for the death of your neighbor. That means you're cruel. There won't be such a thing as cruelty anymore. There'll be neither lovers, nor traitors, nor daredevils, nor true friends, nor prodigal sons.
OLD MAN: What can we do, then?
IVAN: The great human feelings are regarded as cheap and worthless nowadays. You ask what can be done. Now you there, I mean the electrical engineer, listen to what I have to say. You know how an electric light bulb suddenly goes out. Burned out, you'd say ...
VIC: Yeh, burned out ...
IVAN: But say you shake the burned-out bulb?
VIC (*eagerly*): It lights up again.
VERY DRUNK GUEST: Right.
IVAN: It'll light up again and burn for a little while longer. A breakdown's taken place inside the bulb. The filaments have snapped. What are they ...
VIC: Tungsten ...
IVAN: The tungsten filaments have snapped, and when, the fragments come into contact, the light comes back to life ... briefly, unnaturally ...
VIC (*delighted*): Unnaturally.
IVAN: But there's no hiding the fact that its life is doomed. It's like a fever, it burns too brightly. A flash of brilliance, then total darkness. But the momentary brilliance is exquisite. (*A pause.*) You ask: What should we do? Now I'm going to tell you. You must shake the light. You must shake the heart of the burned-out epoch. You must shake this heart like a bulb, so that the fragments will come into contact and blaze up with an exquisite momentary brilliance.
VIC (*spellbound*): Exquisite brilliance.
IVAN: Yes, we're dying. Victims of history ... we're dying ... the nineteenth century is dying, but we're still alive. Our death pangs will be terrible. History, I want to say to you: here's a lover, here's a fool, here's a mother doting on her daughter ... here's a proud man, here's a cheat – here they all are, spokesmen for the great feelings ... (*A pause.*) I want to gather a great horde around me – only then will I be able to make my choice. I go from house to house, searching. Love, where are you?

VIC: Here I am, right here ... that's me, I'm the one who wants to love! ...
IVAN: Vanity, where are you?
ZINOCHKA: Mama, that's me, I'm the one he's calling ... I want great fame ... I want ...
IVAN: Come to me. Love ... be jealous ... be proud ... Be cruel and tender ... Let's go. I'm going to show you to my brother. He makes fun of people like you – of your sauce pans and kettles, of your flower pots, of your quiet little lives, of your right to shove a pacifier in your kids' mouths ... what is he trying to tear out of your hearts? Your own home – home, sweet home! He wants to make you outcasts on the barren fields of history. Let's send him straight to hell. Here's my pillow. I'm the king of pillows. You can tell my brother: Let each of us sleep on his own pillow. Keep your hands off our pillows.
LESS VENERABLE OLD MAN: That kind of brother ought to be killed ... (KAVALEROV *raises his head.*)
IVAN: He will be killed. (*Silence.*) I've been going around looking. I've been trying to find a hired assassin to avenge the century. And I've finally found him! (*Kisses* KAVALEROV *on the forehead. Silence.*) Nikolai Kavalerov is going to kill my brother, Andrei. Tomorrow. At the football game. Here's the razor he's going to do it with. (*Pulls the razor out of* KAVALEROV's *pocket.*)
VIC: Slit his throat ... slit his throat ... (MIKHAIL MIKHAILYCH *beams with satisfaction – the party's been a great success.*)
IVAN: Do you hear that, Kavalerov? They're giving you full power. Oh, my poor, dear friend, what anguish you've suffered! Perhaps your moment of glory that you've been dreaming about since childhood has come at last. Don't give up, here's your chance. Approach this mighty deed with the knowledge that a great century, the nineteenth century, gives you its blessing ...
KAVALEROV: But what if the new century curses me? (*The bulb in the lamp suddenly goes out. Panic.*)
VIC: That's nothing serious, it's all right ... it's just burned out ... I'll fix it right away ... it's nothing ... it's just burned out ...
LADY OF THE HOUSE (*screams*): Shake it! ... Shake it! (*The door opens. Silhouetted in the doorway, with the light behind him,* ANDREI BABICHEV *appears – a huge stone guest. General uproar and then silence.*)
ANDREI: Excuse me, does Citizen Shapiro live here? Solomon Davidovich Shapiro?
LADY OF THE HOUSE (*relieved, almost with a groan*): No, that's higher up, on the third floor (*The door closes. Darkness.*)
KAVALEROV (*hurls himself at the door, bumping into the table and knocking dishes to the floor*): Andrei Petrovich!! Oh, you've gone already!! ...

Oh, you don't want to ... Well, all right ... it's your own fault then ... You're the one that wanted it this way ... (*He calms down. A pause.*)

IVAN: And so, my friends, we'll meet tomorrow at the stadium (*The table's set up on its legs again.*)

(*Curtain.*)

Scene 7
"I Murdered My Own Past"

(*The Stadium. The football game is just about to begin. Bright sunny day. Posters with huge lettering. Greenery, pennants. Refreshment stand, small tables. Picket fences, pathways. Seated at one of the small refreshment tables:* MIKHAIL MIKHAILYCH, ZINOCHKA, *and the* VENERABLE OLD MAN, *all from Scene 6.*)

ZINOCHKA: Is he really going to kill him?
MIKHAIL MIKHAILYCH: Yes, he's going to. There's been so much talk about it. If he doesn't, he'll really be a skunk ...
VENERABLE OLD MAN: Listen ... isn't this dangerous? ... Well, I don't know quite how to say it ... but they won't arrest us as accomplices, will they? ...
MIKHAIL MIKHAILYCH: Why would they? It's not really a crime – it's a murder of historical necessity: one man kills another without any personal motive whatsoever.
VENERABLE OLD MAN: He what? I suppose he'll wear a disguise. He'll probably wear a false mustache ...
ZINOCHKA: But say his mustache suddenly fell off ... that would really be embarrassing. (IVAN BABICHEV *appears with his pillow and* KAVALEROV.)
MIKHAIL MIKHAILYCH: Ssh ... Here they are ... Sssh ... They're not wearing any make-up ... Come over and join us, Ivan Petrovich ...
IVAN: Greetings, my friends ...
MIKHAIL MIKHAILYCH (*to the* WAITER): Waiter! Two dishes of ice cream. (*To* IVAN.) What kind do you want? Raspberry?
IVAN: Yes, raspberry ...
ZINOCHKA: And I'll have the same.
MIKHAIL MIKHAILYCH: And lemon for me. We're in a bit of a hurry. (*Silence.*)
ZINOCHKA (*to* KAVALEROV): Aren't you afraid? Tell me ...

MIKHAIL MIKHAILYCH: Don't interfere, Zinaida Mikhailovna. Don't interfere, or you'll spoil everything ...
IVAN: You look pale, Kavalerov. That won't do.
KAVALEROV: I'm completely calm.
IVAN: You've read Shakespeare, haven't you, Kavalerov? Remember? Remember how Hamlet ends? Corpses, dire passions, misery, and suddenly enter Fortinbras. Enter the conqueror. And all passions come to an end. Enough is enough. Enter Fortinbras – who doesn't give a damn for passions or anguish. All soliloquies are over. Now begin the cheers and fanfares ... (*A pause.*) There ... look, Kavalerov. (*He points to the grandstand with a sweeping gesture.*) Now Fortinbras is going to enter, now the football players are going to enter, and they don't give a damn for your anguish or passions. We've got to hurry, Kavalerov ... Let's go, my friends ... We'll meet him at the entrance ... (*They go out.*)
OLD MAN (*tagging along after them*): Maybe we shouldn't after all. Heavens, maybe it's not worth it ... (*A military band starts playing. ANDREI, HARMAN – a German businessman – and REPRESENTATIVES of the Food Producers Union come on stage. They sit down at one of the small tables on the other side of the refreshment stand.*)
ANDREI: The football game today is sponsored by the Food Producers Union in honor of a new kind of salami which has just come out. Here are the representatives of the Food Producers Union. (*He points them out.*) This is Herr Harman from Berlin, he's a leading authority on nutrition for the masses. (*They bow to one another.*) Herr Harman knows our language. So if you start making wisecracks about his being a dirty capitalist, it'll be pretty embarrassing. (*To* HARMAN.) A man from our firm, Solomon Davidovich Shapiro, should be here at any moment with a sample of the salami.
HARMAN (*makes a great effort to speak correctly*): Oh, you'll have to cut a little piece for me.
ANDREI: We'll make you a whole sandwich. Unfortunately, there's been a slight delay. You see, today's game isn't just a sports event, it's part of an advertising campaign too.
HARMAN: So I've heard. I just heard about it. Someone came out into the umpire's box and shouted through a megaphone that the salami will be on sale tomorrow in all the stores and food stands ...
ANDREI: Yeah, that's the plan ... and we're really sorry that we're a little late in getting it out. But in the meantime, it would be a good idea after today's game to treat the winning team to a couple of pounds of salami. What are you smiling at, Fessenkov?
FESSENKOV: At the offer you just made.

ANDREI: You ought to be ashamed in front of our foreign visitors. You see, Herr Harman, even in the Soviet Union we still haven't been able to get rid of the trappings that went along with medieval tournaments. For example: here's a union man Fessenkov, who's convinced that you can only shower the winning team with roses ...

HARMAN: That's no good, Citizen Fessenkov ...

ANDREI: Es ist nicht gut, Herr Fessenkov ... our salami is just as good as any roses. Herr Harman, we'll make you a rose sandwich ...

HARMAN: Oh, you're a real poet ...

ANDREI: Did you hear that, Safranov? You thought that I was just a salami salesman but it turns out that I'm a poet. O.K. ... Tomorrow we'll show Mr. Harman where they're building "The Quarter." "The Quarter" will open in November. Herr Harman, we're paving the way for a great migration of the masses. That Fessenkov's smirking again. Stop smiling. I'm a poet, and can't help expressing myself this way. Yes, we're paving the way for a great migration of the masses.

HARMAN: Just where do the people have to migrate to?

ANDREI: To the wonderful land of public nutrition. The name of this country is "The Quarter"! What we're trying to do now is make the way to this new land as appealing as possible. There'll be banners to greet the newcomers: "The Quarter Cigarettes," "The Quarter Soap," "The Quarter Fruit Drops." And we're only sorry that we can't sell our salami at less than 35 kopecks a kilo. (*Suddenly getting angry.*) Why doesn't Shapiro come? Where's Shapiro? Why isn't he here? Herr Harman, at "The Quarter" there'll be a schnitzel conveyer belt ...

HARMAN: You're a great cook, Herr Babichev. (*Sees* SHAPIRO *approaching.*) But look, there's someone coming – it must be Shapiro. He's carrying a package.

ANDREI (*bellowing*): Yeah, that's him all right. Over here ... over here ... hurry up, Herr Shapiro ... we're waiting ... we're waiting ... we're waiting ...

SHAPIRO (*comes up to them*): I hurried as fast as I could. I'm awfully hot, Andrei Petrovich ... I brought her. (*Puts the package down on the table.*)

ANDREI: All right, gentlemen, your attention please. Herr Harman, there she is. That's the salami. Der Wurst. Hello, Shapiro. Come here and let me give you a big hug. Quiet, comrades. (*No one's making any noise except* ANDREI.) Take out your notebook now, Herr Harman, and start writing. (*As if he were dictating.*) "Genosse Shapiro brachte Wurst." Write that down. Have you written it down? Now to continue ... "When they first brought it in, I thought it was a rose ..."

HARMAN: "But it was a salami they brought" ... Oh, Herr Babichev, you're just like one little child ...
ANDREI: Keep on writing ... "Then I inhaled a beautiful fragrance" ... (*No longer dictating.*) You know, Herr Harman ... that's a Shakespearean salami ...
SHAPIRO: 70% pure romance ... that is, veal ...
HARMAN: In Russian, are romance and veal really the same thing? I don't know what to write down ...
ANDREI: Write this down: "I saw salami made out of romance, and romance made out of veal" ...
HARMAN: What I'll write is that I don't understand a thing ...
ANDREI: And besides that, write this down: "I saw a mad salami salesman" ... How would you say that in German ...
SHAPIRO: In German that would be: "You're a great guy, Comrade Babichev!"
HARMAN (*speaks in German*): Ach, ja ...
ANDREI: And now, Shapiro, give me a knife ...
SHAPIRO: That's going to be difficult, since I don't have one ... (*Enter IVAN and KAVALEROV, with a CROWD OF FOLLOWERS behind them.*)
IVAN (*on seeing ANDREI*): There he is ... Are you ready, Kavalerov? (KAVALEROV *remains silent.*) Kavalerov, you've got to slam the door hard ... Kavalerov, you've got to leave a scar on history's ugly mug ...
VALYA (*running in on the upper platform*): Andrei Petrovich ... the game's beginning ...
KAVALEROV: I'm ready ... I'm coming ... they'll probably shoot me ... (VALYA *runs down the ramp,* KAVALEROV *climbs up the ramp and meets* VALYA.)
VALYA: Hello, Kavalerov.
KAVALEROV: Hello ...
VALYA: What's the matter with you, Kavalerov? You're not mad at me, are you, because I slapped you?
KAVALEROV: I'm not mad at you, Valya. Are you Andrei Petrovich's wife?
VALYA: Not yet ...
KAVALEROV: I'm just about to slit his throat with a razor ...
VALYA: You? Well, then go ahead and slit it ... Andrei Petrovich ...
KAVALEROV: Valya ...
VALYA: Andrei Petrovich, Kavalerov's come to slit your throat ...
ANDREI: Who, me? Now? ... here? ... O.K. ... What am I supposed to do? Lie down? Unbutton my collar?
SHAPIRO: Well, now we're going to have a little Shakespeare ...

ANDREI: What would you like to cut my throat with?
VALYA: A razor.
ANDREI: Well, let's start cutting then, Kavalerov. (*He takes the razor from* KAVALEROV *and starts to cut the salami.*) That's the way we slice it ... smell the aroma? ...
IVAN: Cut his throat! ... down with salami salesmen! Cut his throat ...
KAVALEROV: No, that's not it ... give me the razor ... (KAVALEROV *snatches the razor out of* ANDREI's *hands and heads for* IVAN.)
ZINOCHKA: Stop him ...
IVAN: I see now, I see ... (*All of* IVAN's FOLLOWERS *retreat in horror.* IVAN *runs offstage. A moment later he lets out a terrible shriek.*)
KAVALEROV (*runs in from offstage*): There, I've killed him ... I've murdered my own past ... let me explain ...
ANDREI: That's the end of the old passions ... The new world is beginning. (*A whistle. The* FOOTBALL PLAYERS *come down the ramp.*)

(*Curtain.*)

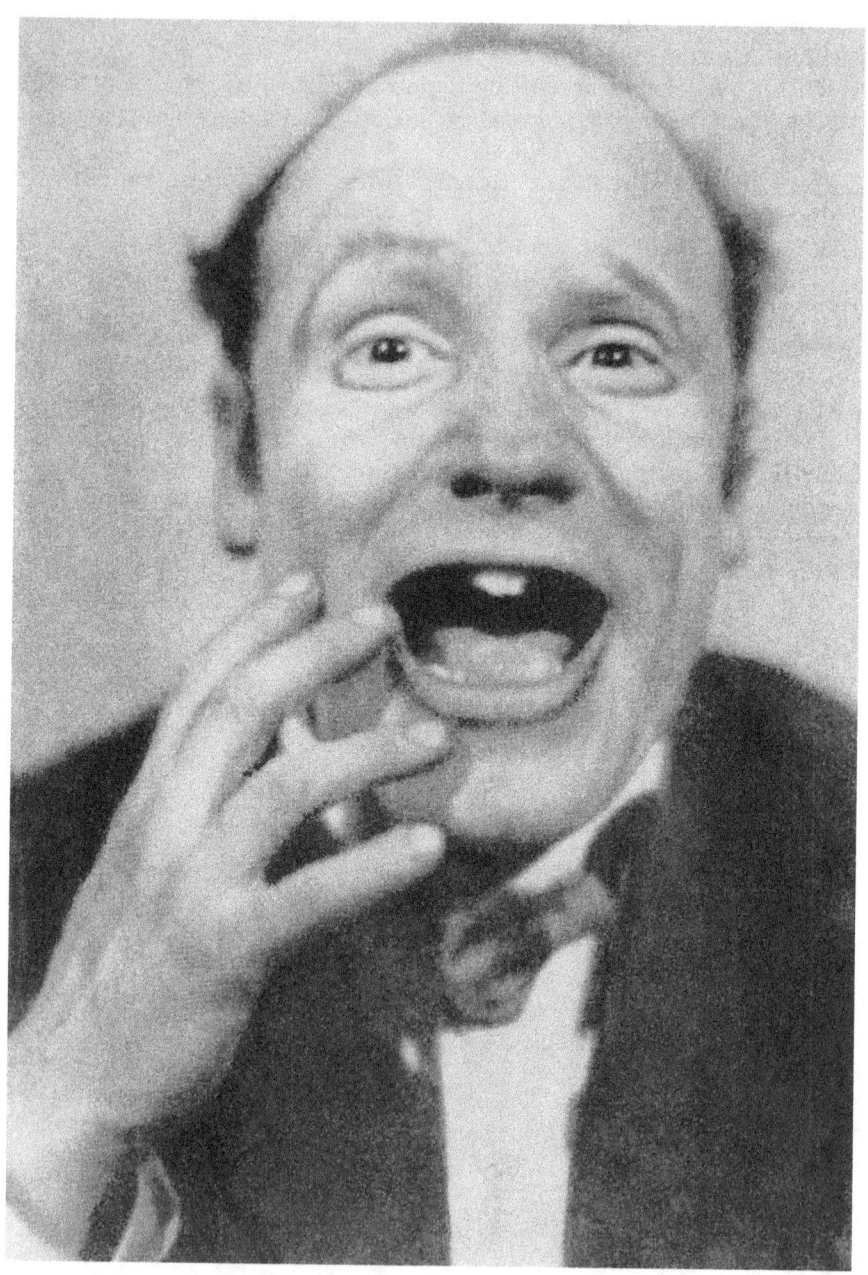

1. Ivan Babichev — A. Goryunov
   Vakhtangov Theatre 1929

2. Shapiro — B. Shchukin
   Vakhtangov Theatre, 1929

3. Valya — E. Alekseeva
   Vakhtangov Theatre, 1929

4. *The Conspiracy of Feelings*: Scene 2 — the communal kitchen
   Directed by Aleksi Popov, designed by Nikolai Akimov
   Vakhtangov Theatre, 1929

5. *The Conspiracy of Feelings*: Scene 3 — Ivan and Andrei Babichev (O. Glazunov)
   Vakhtangov Theatre, 1929

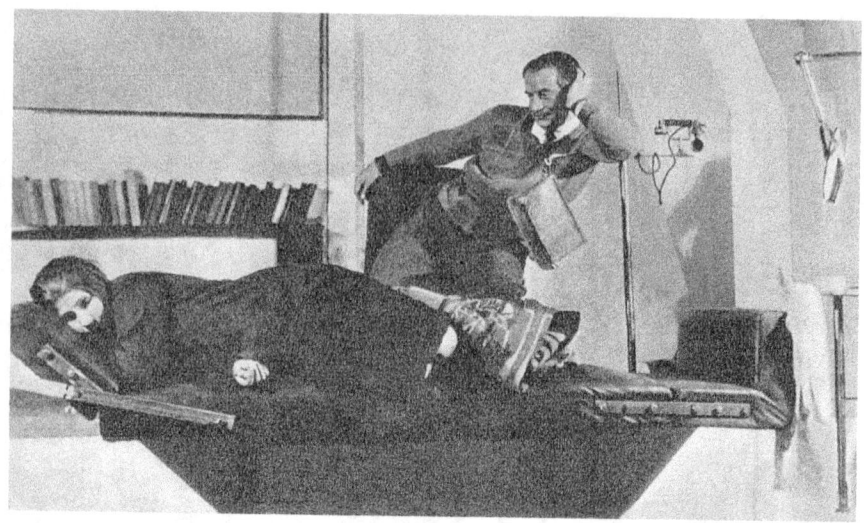

6. *The Conspiracy of Feelings*: Scene 3 — Andrei Babichev (O. Glazunov), Valya (E. Alekseeva) Vakhtangov Theatre, 1929

7. *The Conspiracy of Feelings*: Scene 4 — Ivan, Valya, Shapiro, Andrei Vakhtangov Theatre, 1929

8. *The Conspiracy of Feelings*: Scene 5 — Kavalerov's dream
   Kavalerov — V. Moskvin
   Vakhtangov Theatre, 1929

9. *The Conspiracy of Feelings*: Scene 6 — the Name Day Party
   Vakhtangov Theatre, 1929

10. *The Conspiracy of Feelings*: Scene 7 — the Stadium
    Vakhtangov Theatre, 1929

Appendix

"The Author about his Play: For the Production of *The Conspiracy of Feelings* at the Bolshoi Dramatic Theatre"
(*The Life of Art* [Leningrad], No. 52, 1929)

My play *The Conspiracy of Feelings*, now playing in Moscow at the Vakhtangov Theatre, is an adaptation of my novel *Envy*.

This I can say about my play: like any play derived from a work of fiction, it has certain faults – it is long and drawn-out in places, the plot is not properly worked out, and it is too wordy.

If I had written a play on the same subject as the story, but without having the story as its source, the play would have turned out completely differently and been completely unlike *The Conspiracy of Feelings* in structure and far superior to it.

The theme of the play is the struggle for passionate commitment. A young man, Nikolai Kavalerov, who is just as old as the century is, enters into the struggle with his "benefactor" Andrei Babichev – a communist and a director of a food industry trust.

Kavalerov considers Andrei a blockhead, a "salami salesman," a graven image, devoid of feelings, a machine that stifles everything human: tenderness, genuine feeling, individuality.

The young man dreams of becoming "the hired assassin avenging his century." He wants to kill the communist Andrei Babichev, in order not to surrender without a fight to this new figure and give up his own personality which he considers highly gifted and undeservedly doomed to destruction.

A conspiracy grows up against the director. At the head of the conspiracy stands the director's brother, a fantastic character, Ivan Babichev, the king of pillows: "Follow Me! All you cowards, jealous ones, lovers, heroes … you knights in shining armor … follow me … I'll lead you on our last march."

Thus cries the king.

The hired assassin raises his hand. He must leave a scar "on history's ugly mug."

My aim was to show that passionate involvement is not the exclusive monopoly of people from the old world, that strong feeling is not just showing off and ranting and raving, that those building the new world and a new way of life are more humane than anyone else and that what seems to the condemned man to be the stone face of a graven image is really the shining face of the new man, incomprehensible to the one who is condemned, threatening and blinding him.

A whole series of accusations were leveled against me on account of the central figure, Andrei Babichev. He is a sausage-maker – according to the criticisms – a sausage-maker and nothing more. I deliberately gave my communist-hero an odd profession to make him theatrical and alive. Then, to counterbalance the dazzling talk of the people from the past, I wanted to make the hero's diction rough and ironic, and I wanted to contrast plain salami with Ophelias and concrete reality with vague romanticism.

Let people who still live in the past fly into a rage, boil over, and get furious because the new man has the ability to be a poet of salami.

Living is more frightening when one has nothing to live for. It is all the more frightening for Kavalerov to experience the collapse of his romanticism when he sees it break on such an unromantic thing as salami.

What concerns me most of all is whether my play is "intelligible" to the masses. The Bolshoi Dramatic Theatre is now working on the play to make it intelligible. I think that the theatre will be successful.

"Notes of a Dramatist" (1933, published in *Collected Works*, Moscow, 1956)

1) I am interested in the question of the physical destruction of characters in plays.

In the past plays were written in which the participants were kings, princes, generals, knights (Shakespeare, Schiller, Hugo). It was an easy matter for these characters to destroy one another. They all wore swords, and – at the slightest provocation – a sword was quickly drawn, and the murder required by the plot took place.

Poison too was often used. Poison was poured into the hero's goblet. Or the hero poured poison into someone else's goblet. Poison was prepared by court doctors. They kept it in a ring.

Although it may seem comical, the question of the right to bear arms exerts some influence on the techniques of playwriting.

Let us consider plays written in the pre-revolutionary period. For example, Chekhov's plays. Chekhov could not conceive of a play without a shot. A shot rings out in all his plays. In the vaudeville *The Bear* the action revolves around pistols. And even in the well-known formulation of the laws of drama, Chekhov could not get along without firearms: "If a gun hangs on the wall in the first act, then it must be fired in the last."

Ivanov shoots himself, Voinitsky shoots Serebryakov, Treplev shoots himself. A duel takes place in *The Three Sisters*. Incidentally, it is interesting to note that Chekhov was somewhat embarrassed by the flashiness of a shot on stage. He reduces this flashiness in several cases. For example, when Voinitsky shoots at Professor Serebryakov, he shouts "bang" as he does it. It is not a real shot, Chekhov indicates, not a shot producing thunder and lightning, but only a "bang." It is a restrained, non-combatant, comical shot (but a shot all the same). There is the same kind of reduction in *The Seagull*. The sound of the shot is like the sound of a can of ether exploding.

In the bourgeois era it was easy to buy a weapon in a store. There is a story of Chekhov's in which a deceived husband picks out a weapon in a store. And Ivanov came to his own wedding with a revolver.

The last stage direction in *Ivanov* reads: "Ivanov runs to one side and shoots himself." That means, before going to his own wedding, a man pulled a revolver out of his desk and put it in the pocket of his dress pants.

That is how simply things were done then.

But what about us?

The right to bear arms is under strict control, and this right is granted to just those people who are least likely to do any shooting for personal reasons.

Most often we have recourse to a secondary issue: the theft of the revolver.

In this connection there are certain difficulties occasioned by life itself. When, let us suppose X decides to kill Y, he makes a special trip to Leningrad to his brother's and steals a revolver from him. The trip to Leningrad, the theft of the revolver – that's a whole act of the play!

A person can be killed with a chair or an axe as well as with a gun. But such murders do not occur on the stage, since they are not convincing. In Andreev's

Thought, Kerzhentsev uses a paper-weight to kill someone. But Andreyev indicates that the man who gets murdered stands there as though he were hypnotized, and the murderer brings down his hand in a slow, jerky fashion. Thus it is extremely important for Andreyev to fix the actor's attention at this point. In this instance the dramatist realizes that it is impossible for the murderous blow to come off convincingly.

In a drama, everything is constructed around the sufferings of some character, and the action eventually comes to the point where this character either kills, is killed, or kills himself. Every drama contains some external criminal act. It is very difficult to recall a drama without the actual death of one of the characters.

In our Soviet plays, if a character pulls out a revolver, the question immediately arises: Where did he get the revolver?

A dramatist jots down in his notebook: "Next he is going to shoot him." That is rash. To avoid falsehood and stretching things, first it is necessary to work out carefully how, where, and by what means the weapon came into the characters possession.

Now the following idea occurs to me: our Soviet playwriting more than any other offers the possibility of dramas in which destruction is brought about by a logic machine. Physical destruction becomes logical destruction. Man is transformed not into a corpse, but a zero.

2) Money was the principal theme in bourgeois drama. The theme of money, of getting rich. Especially getting rich suddenly. Wealth was the reward for inner qualities. The material standard of wealth had to be improved and raised.

A promissory note. How often it turns up in bourgeois plays! It is crumpled, torn, burned. It is wept over, given back, stolen. It holds the plot together, creates the conflicts, emerges as part of a triangle, constituting the drama itself. The struggle centers around it. It is the litmus paper revealing the truth in people.

Or, for example, the rich suitor. There used to be rich suitors. In novels you would come across sentences such as:

"He was one of the richest suitors in Russia."

What does that mean? What is a "rich suitor"? We do not know, we do not know. Now there aren't any rich matches any more. Now even the word "suitor" is going out of style. Now it is extremely rare to hear the phrase:

– He is her suitor.

A rich suitor was one of the most effective characters in bourgeois drama. His entrance received a long preparation, he would not appear until the end of the act.

It was awful to live in those times! In order to get a blessing for one's marriage from some important relative – a distant relative who ignored one's pleas, but who was the most important and wealthiest, how long one had to wait and grovel. Five whole acts!

For there used to be the concept: inheritance. I.e., money. I.e., getting rich.

Inheritance. It was essential to obtain one. To wait for an inheritance ... Oh! It is a struggle, a duel, a source of the most fascinating characters. Forgers of wills. Kidnappers of children. Secrets, secrets, secrets. What complications, what crises, what meetings in the last act, what tears, what capes on footmen, what tearing off of masks!

In the bourgeois world, everyone has the "opportunity" to make his own fortune in the world. You could make a million. You could find a bag full of money. That world made the theme of money magical. The dream of suddenly getting rich was transformed into the captivating images of Cinderella and the Ugly Duckling. That world created the type of the foundling, the type of the thief who stole for the sake of the poor, the type of the benevolent rich man. Little by little, imperceptibly, insidiously money – as the chief motive of all of life – took root in art.

This theme – the theme of money – became very firmly established in art and captured the imagination of artists. It began to give birth to such ideal and angelic figures that one even lost sight of how cruelly materialistic, dirty, and bloody this theme was.

How fascinating Jean Valjean is in Hugo's *Les Misérables*. He changed from a thief into a rich man. He changed from a convict into an honest man. A benevolent rich man, he saved a little girl from want and degradation. He met her that night in the forest. She was carrying a heavy bucket. As they were walking along, he took the bucket from her hand; suddenly she stopped feeling the weight – he carried the bucket which weighed down the poor little beggar girl. A tavern keeper and his wife – crooks, evil rich people – humiliated the girl. The benevolent rich man took her part and punished them. Externally, aesthetically, this sounds unusually powerful. Remember that scene ... Thus the theme of getting rich in bourgeois art gave birth to both strong emotions and the tenderest melodies.

In our Soviet world, where private property is dying out, the theme of getting rich is disappearing. It is disappearing forever, like smoke, dispersing never to arise again, it is dead and buried. The myth of Cinderella cannot be repeated.

In America they say:

– That man is worth two million.

A different evaluation of man interests us: in a society where there will be neither rich nor poor, to have the opportunity to determine the absolute value of man. In a classless society much will be done to improve man. Competition arises in this connection. Which of us is better, purer, more intelligent, more creative? Whose value is higher?

Absolute value. Without millions. Without an inheritance.

Perhaps this aspect – competition among human qualities – will become the main theme of playwriting in the future.

And such competition will certainly create the sharpest conflicts and could be very tragic. But its purpose is pure and high: to become better.

3) People say: a fascinating person.

There are fascinating people. There are people without fascination – totally good, intelligent, well-educated, honest, affable, but devoid of the ability to attract others sympathetically.

There are people with whom you don't want to leave the party when it's time to go home, people you want to get away from.

But I am convinced that for everyone – even for a completely undistinguished, ordinary person, there is a sphere of activity where he becomes fascinating.

I've noticed that people become fascinating while they are executing a job, that is, when they are making movements each of which is necessary and useful. That is, people moving in rhythm. It is always pleasant to see people with hammers repairing the street car at night. The driver becomes fascinating as he focuses all his attention.

One day the wire for the streetcar broke. They roped off the place. The streetcar stopped. The crowd was quiet. Then the emergency repair tower arrived. A young man wearing gloves appeared at the top, above the crowd – he did something with the wire. He was all concentration. And, without even knowing it – or rather, without having time to think of it – he was an actor in front of a large number of spectators. And everyone looked at him with delight and admiration, feeling some gratitude to him and at the same time envy and the wish to be like him and to be able to be proud of him. That is, they experienced the kind of feelings which arise when you are in love.

A man directing the lethally dangerous traffic of transport vehicles has to show the utmost in concentration. He is responsibility personified. Not one superfluous movement. In this lies his gracefulness and in the fact that he becomes someone we want to imitate.

This is the point which explains how life itself, without the artist's intervention, can become art.

When he appears at the scene of an accident, the doctor has great magical powers of fascination. This terrible figure extracting glittering steel from a little satchel, this possessor of momentary but superhuman greatness, who calls for stretcher-bearers with a movement of his finger, after feeling the pulse of the person lying in the road without saying anything to the crowd about the condition of the victim – this man is the personification of what is loudly proclaimed as life and death.

The favorable responses called forth by the figure of a great surgeon are well known.

The child does not die out in people. There is an element of play in a military parade. There is an element of play in the mounting of the guard; in the ceremonies of congresses and law courts. And how frightfully these things, which call forth love in children, are linked with death and blood!

Scenes of arrest, scenes of interrogation, scenes of trial – how effective they are in plays, how the public loves them!

It seems to me that the figure who appears in the play and says, Don't be afraid, is the most fascinating one. The person to whom the fearful come for help produces a catch in the audience's throat by his every word and gesture. The figure of the protector. He is a relation of that young man wearing gloves in the emergency repair tower who makes every movement with the utmost care and efficiency as he repairs the broken wire, since even the slightest contact with it could kill him.

4) When I was a boy, they used to sell a wonderful kind of transfers. They came in a little book or album. Various scenes were depicted on the pages, painted in a single shade – a dark color.

It seemed natural to imagine that when the transfer was made onto paper the same scene would appear, only bright and multicolored.

But – and this was the specialty of that sort of little picture – a completely different picture came out on the paper, incredibly bright, new, surprising, coming from no one knew where.

One of these pictures I remembered all my life. I did not know what it was all about then. I only found out much later.

It was an episode dealing with the suppression of the Boxer Rebellion in China. There was a high wall beneath an indescribably blue sky, and from the wall were hanging decapitated Chinese. And blood – indescribably scarlet – was running down the wall. The little picture glistened because it had just come out of the water.

I was very young then: only six or seven. I wrote my first poetry at seventeen. Consequently, I did not even have any idea for a long time that I would ever be involved with art. But I remember clearly that the impression which I got from contemplating that amazing picture has stood out sharply from all other impressions of childhood.

I became convinced at that moment that space and time are relative, that there is in this world an opportunity to control this relativity and that the opportunity to control this relativity resides in art. This small picture, the size of a playing card, could not be evaluated by its dimensions alone. It entered one's consciousness as the event itself, and not as the portrayal of the event.

Of course, I only analyzed this phenomenon much later, but that it was extremely strange, new, and even shocking – all that I recognized already when I was a child at the very moment that this phenomenon arose.

I was not able to carry on such a reflections then, but still the shadow of a thought passed through my mind – the thought that the essence of drama lies in the interrelationships between space and man (the small Chinamen, the wall, and the empty sky), i.e. in the composition.

That was my first acquaintance with art. Childhood impressions have a special significance for the later development of an artist's relationship to the world. When I'm writing a play or preparing to work on one, as I ponder what kind of outer form my new idea will take, I always relive the memory of the transfer, I see it shining before me. It was brilliantly staged – space, figures, and properties were all marvelously arranged in it. In it there was the air of the dramatic event.

5) I want to write a play in which one of the main characters will be an egotist.

The type of person in love with himself.

The egotist lives in a large room with two windows. Nice furniture, a bright hallway, trees and grass nearby. At the windows, which open on the garden, there is a delightful atmosphere created by the reflections of sky and greenery, the shadows of the glass, the smells. The egotist steps into these surroundings. He goes to the closet. The closet is between the windows. The egotist doesn't notice the difference between one kind of atmosphere and another. Meanwhile the green light from the tree, which spread its branches beyond the window, flies into the room, and the egotist's hands turn green. His shirt turns green too. The egotist doesn't suspect for a moment that it is anything but snowy white.

The tree grows just a stone's throw from the window. It is young and strong. The egotist doesn't notice: after taking a nap the tree stretches, yawns, and shakes itself.

The egotist opens the closet. It is totally dark in the closet. The neckties are shimmering. He selects a necktie. He ties the necktie, looking in the mirror below. He knows – the mirror can last forever, if it doesn't get broken. It almost defies time, it doesn't age. The durability of "Gillette" razor blades is nothing in comparison to the mirror. The egotist reflects: "For my lifetime, one mirror and two closets are enough, but how many razor blades?"

The egotist still has about forty years to live. He says to himself: "I'm thirty-five, I've had a new fur coat made. It will last me ten years." He doesn't reflect any further. But one could reflect further along these lines: ten years will pass, the beaver fur will get thin, the hairs will fall out, the cloth will become threadbare, the polecat skin will wear out. I'll have to have a new coat made. That will happen in ten years. But something else will happen in ten years. Not only will the fur coat wear out, so will the person wearing it – his hair will fall out, his skin will wrinkle. They'll say of him: he went through a child's winter coat, a schoolboy's overcoat, a university student's overcoat and beyond that even two excellent fur coats. The second half of his life was made up of two excellent fur coats. The second fur coat lasted until his death. We're catching the egotist in the period of his first fur coat. It's his heyday, the high point for him. The fur coat is magnificent.

As a large unit of his life is composed of smaller ones, so the fur coat of the egotist, which we took as the large unit of his life, also consists of smaller units: suits, separate pairs of pants, shirts, hats, lap rugs, crystal glasses. And as the days in a century flash by, so many that they cannot be counted, so rapidly they cannot be noticed, so too the "Gillette" razor blades flash by, innumerable and imperceptible in the fur coat-century.

The egotist is encased in the beautiful. The limit of human sight lies in infinity. We see the starry nebulae. The limit of the egotist's sight is confined to exactly that swing of the arm necessary to slide his arm into the sleeve of his fur coat.

So the character of the egotist is prepared for.

He has a hard pink bald spot. He is handsome and smells of perfume. Once he dropped a ten-kopeck piece in the streetcar. You can imagine it for yourself: he dropped the ten-kopeck piece in the streetcar just at the exit, just as the car came to a stop, when the crowd started pushing. He began to look for the ten-kopeck piece. He looked for it under the passengers' feet, making movements like someone washing the floor.

His behind stuck out. Do you picture it? He kept looking until he got poked in the behind with a fist.

So the egotist lives in the notebook. For the time being he is treated in prose fiction. Next he will begin to act.

He will be the representative of man's power over his fellow man – and he will be punished for it.

Now the process of playwriting and the working out of the characters must begin. The character of the egotist – maybe an excellent citizen, a hard worker, a useful and indispensable man, but a selfish person, an egotist – is to me unusually interesting as a character to portray on the stage.

Alternate Ending to *The Conspiracy of Feelings* by Yurii Olesha

[*The text printed below is Olesha's original version. During the course of rehearsals, the playwright changed the ending to the version given above.*]

HARMAN (*speaks in German*): Ach, ja ... (IVAN *approaches followed by the* CROWD.) Who's that man? What's he doing here with a pillow? Maybe he wants to move the land of the collective kitchen?

IVAN: Andryusha, treat me to some salami. (*Silence.*) Mr. Harman, write this down: a crazy sausage-maker stole his own brother's daughter.

HARMAN: Mr. Babichev, this is an advertisement too. (*Silence.*)

ANDREI: If you don't get out of here immediately, I'll have you arrested.

IVAN: They'll let me go. I'm harmless. I'm not a magician, Andryusha, I'm a trickster. And here's the last trick: the flying sausage. (*He seizes the salami, swings his arms, general panic, throws the salami in* ANDREI's *face. He grows frightened himself.*) Bravo, bravo. War's declared. Down with Andrei, the sausage-maker. Great. Well, what are going to do? Grab me. (*They try to grab him. He runs away. He holds the pillow like a defensive weapon.*) Kavalerov, Kavalerov. Cut his throat. Long live the conspiracy of feelings. Slash him. Slash him. (*They grab him, the pillow rolls away.* KAVALEROV *climbs up to the group.* VALYA *appears.* IVAN *starts struggling violently as they hold him.*) Here he comes. You see. He'll kill you. Aha ... you're going pale. You're scared, Andryusha. (KAVALEROV *climbs up. He has his razor in his hand. He notices* VALYA.)

VALYA: That's not true. We're not afraid. Don't be afraid. Don't be afraid. (KAVALEROV *drops his razor, looks back, makes an attempt to pick it up, can't, sits down on the steps.*)

KAVALEROV: Well ... now please give me a minute of your attention ... Andrei Petrovich, I raised my hand against you ... and I can't ... condemn me ... punish me ... put out my eyes ... I want to be blind ... I've got to be blind so I won't see you ... and your triumph ... and your world ...

VALYA: Andrei Petrovich, we've got to finish this. The football players are coming. (*In run* VIC, *the* WOMAN IN GREEN, *the* VERY DRUNK GUEST, *and the* LESS VENERABLE OLD MAN.)

VIC (*seeing* KAVALEROV *lying on the steps*): Oh, we're too late. He's killed himself.

IVAN: He's alive. He's alive. He's not dead. He's a stuffed animal. He's a doll. Take Kavalerov off to the museum. Bring the doll to the museum. Bring the man whose life they stole to the museum.

ANDREI: Take them away. The match is beginning. (*A march. The* FOOTBALL PLAYERS *come down the ramp. Twenty-two men in brightly colored uniforms.*)

Anatolii Lunacharsky, "The Conspiracy of Feelings," Krasnaya Gazeta, March 23, 1929

The Vakhtangov Theatre, each of whose productions is a great theatrical event, took Olesha's play *The Conspiracy of Feelings* and created yet another staging of immense cultural value.

Olesha's novel *Envy* attracted broad attention. A great deal was written about it. No one doubted its exceptional merit, but the purpose of the novel elicited doubts. At first glance, its meaning was totally clear: the central character, the seedy intellectual Kavalerov, was considered the bearer of the feeling of burning envy toward the new Bolshevik world and its representatives.

But on closer examination it became evident that Kavalerov and his ally, Ivan Babichev, who functioned as the guiding force behind all the turmoil caused by the old world's envy of the new, were developed not only with much knowledge of their inner lives, but also with a certain sympathy. The critics began to wonder: given the complex psychology noted by the author and the partially valid discontent of the representatives of nineteenth-century culture, won't some readers find the scales tipped in their favor, while on the other side the Bolshevik characters (Andrei Babichev, Volodya Makarov) are shown to be not so much inspired by the revolutionary struggle as serving (granted, wholeheartedly and enthusiastically) various aspects of our economic construction? Some wondered: isn't Olesha displaying an original and instinctive brand of cunning, when he, while amply bespattering Ivan Babichev and Kavalerov with mud, simultaneously delights in the lurid colors of the process of decay consuming them and spares no pains to depict the peculiar brilliance of their decadent experiences, while at the same time in the Bolshevik world opposed to them, Olesha makes salami, "The Quarter," and gymnastics, play such a central role, as if unwittingly reducing to sobriety and prose our building of communism that allows no scope for living human feelings, which indeed cannot be so readily accommodated in pure economy, for example. Other critics wondered if this wasn't what Olesha meant: "The old world is irredeemably condemned and dying; but look what a peculiar richness it had! The new world, of course, will triumph, but those who claimed that its ideal is above all the satisfaction of the stomach are right after all."

Remarks of that sort applied to *Envy* as a novel are incorrect. But I must admit that in adapting it for the stage the author made some important changes. They take two different directions; we completely approve of the first, but have a few reservations about the second.

In giving dramatic form to the same conception as in the novel, the author more sharply stressed the basic lines. Thus the entire subject is simplified in the play.

At the end of the play Kavalerov foments a revolt against his mentor and source of inspiration, Ivan Babichev, exterminating him with his own hands and bowing down before the life principle, embodied by Andrei Babichev. And in true Fortinbras style Andrei proclaims: "That's the end of the old passion" – a march is heard and the football players enter.

For this reason the play has taken on the characteristic of glorifying a bit the communist way of life. The "i's" have been dotted.

We cannot hold this against the author, because, although the rather problematic subject of the novel is explicitly defined in the play, nevertheless the execution of this drama, depicting the collision of two worlds and the victory of the new, is done in such a complex and subtle fashion that the charge of simplification or crude tendentiousness does not touch the play.

But, as if to answer the already voiced criticism of the novel, the author slightly modifies Andrei Babichev's traits.

We'll make a reservation immediately. To demand that the positive hero of a play express some kind of "synthetic communism" and be "a communist from head to toe," in whom the whole gamut of communism is clearly exhibited as a towering social phenomenon, is to demand the impossible or even to lead authors totally astray. There is not and there never could be a communist who would express the totality of all the traits characteristic of communism. This would not be a living human being, or a type, but some strange kind of artificial allegory. No single living communist is a reflection of the entire party or of all the ideas of communism, but only of some of its particular traits, for communism as a party and as an idea is significantly broader than any individual, even the very greatest.

In the novel Andrei Babichev, whom Kavalerov maliciously calls a salami-maker, an operator, and so forth, actually reflects a certain very important, very famous, very triumphant line of communism – namely, the practical building of communism, the enthusiastic dedication to various precise tasks, which, if detached from the overall scheme of all our aspirations, can really seem prosaic, but fidelity and dedication to which in their absolute concreteness seen in relation to the overall plan is, on the contrary, the true pride of communism.

Yes, Andrei Babichev wants to make a delicious, nutritious, cheap salami, yes, he is building a huge cafeteria with the prosaic name, "The Quarter." He is not only in general terms a business executive, he is more precisely a food industry worker. But there is even just cause for his pride in being a genuine communist food industry worker, for whom his concrete tasks are illumined by the bright flame of the battle against the individual kitchen, against the enslavement of woman, against the frightful scourge of house work, which Lenin so branded – by the flame of the battle for the collectivization of alimentation.

By the same token any other economic task that we might undertake, is, as I interpret it, an enormous, grand endeavor worthy of the same whole-hearted dedication.

It is mean, low, and shabby for communists (or more often unwelcome praisers of communism) to begin accusing Andrei Babichev in Kavalerov's style of actually being an operator and a salami maker and suggesting that this character should have been turned into something more synthetic, broad, high, and so forth.

Unfortunately, Olesha seems to have heeded criticism of this sort and to have tried to sentimentalize Andrei Babichev. A play is not life – a character in a drama is not a living human being taken from life, he must be constructed in such a way that the general theme of the play is developed as much as possible. And from this point of view it was necessary to make Andrei a relentless "operator."

If it is made clear that this operator is not out to increase his own capital or to advance his own career, but that he is a Soviet operator, then all that cackling will have no effect on such a character.

As the reader can see, if there are those who reproach Olesha for having made Andrei too prosaic an operator, we reproach him for the opposite. He should have been made a more consistent and ruthless communist-operator. However, in so far as much of this element was present in Andrei anyhow, we consider the character more or less satisfactory.

If Olesha's play in general seems a somewhat flawed, but successful adaptation of his novel, we can speak of the production only in tones of the highest praise.

The second scene, depicting a kind of contemporary Moscow Hoffmanniada in the depths of a densely populated Philistine Moscow apartment, is uncanny and hits the mark in such masterly fashion that one would like to see something of the sort in an entire play, based on just such a forced communal dwelling and, perhaps, developing in these tones an entire dramatic philosophy.

The dream scene, which to many seemed stylized and fantastic, is in actual fact amazingly realistic and triumphantly supreme.

Striking also in both its literary and its theatrical dimensions is the dazzling scene of Ivan Babichev's "Last Supper," in which the petty bourgeois table-companions reveal their repressed feelings and collectively condemn to death the Bolshevik Andrei.

Finally, the last scene, in particular its closing chord, represents a really triumphant finale. It was met with thunderous applause that did not die down for a long time, coming from – almost without exception – the entire audience at the dress rehearsal. *The Conspiracy of Feelings* is a great new victory for the Vakhtangov Theatre and at the same time a great new victory on our whole theatrical front.

Mariya O. Knebel', "My Great Friend," from *Contemporaries on the Creative Work of A. D. Popov: Director, Teacher, Friend. A Collection of Reminiscences* (1966)

It must be said that the production was a stupendous success. The biting, wrathful conception cut like a scalpel into the flaccid but still tenacious and obtuse world view of the petty bourgeoisie.

The weird mask worn by the leader of the conspiracy, Ivan Babichev, was that of a paunchy little man with a flabby face, a philosopher-maniac and court fool. Anatolii Goryunov played the role brilliantly. The yellow pillow, from which Babichev was inseparable, served as a symbol of faith and as the banner of the conspiracy. For good reason Babichev displayed the pillow so tenderly and triumphantly in the splendidly staged name-day scene, which Lunacharsky mentions. The huge oval table was spread with food, like a gigantic trough, around which the guests have gathered to pant, to slurp, to grunt, in short, "to pass the time chicly." In their midst is Babichev. His howl of "Back to the nineteenth century!" calls forth cries of ecstasy and tears of tender emotion. And above all this, like the sun in the sky, hangs a huge lamp shade – idol of petty bourgeois coziness. In this scene the conception of the director and the designer (N. P. Akimov) coincided perfectly and figuratively skewered the auditorium, seeking the philistine in order to smite him down.

With murderous force the director depicted another true beachhead for the operations of the king of vulgarians – the famous communal apartment buildings. In their dirty stairwells covered with cobwebs and the mold of corridors, in their kitchens smoking from the muzzles of primus stoves and oil burners, Babichev's poisonous idea blossomed and found corroboration. Here he is again on the top, above all the others. And down below are the philistines, embittered by many years of communal civil war, family scandals, backbiting, foul air, and chronic diseases. All the house scum crawled out of their corners, dumbfounded by the trance-like state of their prophet.

A. D. Popov emphasized to the maximum the visual characteristics of each inhabitant of the apartment building, gloriously adding them to the construction of "the communal house," deftly and maliciously built by Akimov. The director's concept received its sharpest embodiment in a memorable visual image: blending of the geometric flights of stairs and the intestine-shaped chimney pipe, which appeared from nowhere and disappeared into infinity, with the fractured tenants twisted into various poses.

And then there was Annichka's "realm" – the "realm" of Kavalerov's mistress! Annichka, Kavalerov and Babichev lived in the huge, gigantic bed. Yes, they lived, that is, they quarreled, made malicious remarks, sat, lay, ate, slept, and all that in the bed which was decorated with oval mirrors, sumptuous pillows, and playful cupids. Fantastic wallpaper, painted with concentric circles of paradise apples, decorated the walls of Annichka's "temple" of love.

Here too, in this bedroom Nikolai Kavalerov in a dream choked with an impotent scream. Here unfolded the scene of his visions, which Lunacharsky called "triumphantly supreme."

The naive and sick imagination of Kavalerov peopled the scene with fantastic figures, each of them a witty and accurate find of the director.

The tragic in *The Conspiracy of Feelings* was interwoven with the comic, the comic with the fantastic, and all together created a unique poetic and satiric theatrical element, amazingly coinciding with the world of the complex man and writer Yurii Olesha.

Selective Bibliography

Appel, Sabine. *Jurij Olesa "Zavist" und "Zagovor cuvstv": ein Vergleich des Romans mit seiner dramatisierten Fassung.* Arbeiten und Texte zur Slavistik, 1. München: Sagner, 1973.
Beaujour, Elizabeth. *The Invisible Land. A Study of the Artistic Imagination of Iurii Olesha.* New York: Columbia University Press, 1970.
Harkins, William E. "Jurij Olesa's Drama Zagovor cuvstv" in *Zbirnyk na poshanu prof. d-ra IUriia Shevelova.* Miukhen: Universitas Libera Ucrainensis, 1971.
_____. "Yuri Olesha (1899–1960)" in *European Writers of the Twentieth Century*, ed. George Stade, Vol. 11. New York: Scribners, 1990.
Kirpotin, Valery. "Olesha dramaturg" in *Proza, dramaturgiia, teatr.* Moscow: Khudozhestvennaya Literatura, 1935.
Knebel', Mariya O. "Moi bolshoi drug" in *Sovremenniki o tvorchestve A. D. Popova: rezhisser, uchitel', drug. Sbornik vospominanii.* Ed. Yurii S. Kalashnikov. Moscow: Vserossiiskoe Teatral'noe Obshchestvo, 1966.
Lunacharsky, Anatolii. *O Vahtangove i vakhtangovtsakh.* Moscow: Iskusstvo, 1959.
Pavel Markov. "Yurii Olesha" in *O Teatre. Vol. IV: Dnevnik Teatral'nogo Kritika 1930–1976.* Moscow: Iskusstvo, 1977.
Olesha, Yurii. *P'esy. Stat'i o teatre i dramaturgii.* Introduction by Pavel Markov. Moscow: Iskusstvo, 1968.
_____. *Izbrannoe.* Introduction by Viktor Shklovsky. Moscow: Khudozhestvennaya Literatura, 1974.
Peppard, Victor. *The Poetics of Yury Olesha.* Gainesville: University of Florida Press, 1989.
Pertsov, Viktor O. *My Zhivem vpervye. O tvorchestve Iuriya Oleshi.* Moscow: Sovetskii Pisatel', 1976.
Prigozhina, Larisa. "'Y menya bylo vsego dva etapa …' ("Ironicheskaya drama" i "pateticheskaya melodrama" Yuriya Oleshi)" in *Problemy poeticheskoi dramy i sovetskii teatr.* Leningrad: Ministerstvo Kul'tury RSFSR, 1991.

Introduction to *The Little Theatre of the Green Goose*
Daniel Gerould

Konstanty Ildefons Gałczyński (1905–1953), one of Poland's most beloved and popular poets, began his career in the mid-1920s writing humorous verse and fantastic stories. Mobilized as a soldier at the outbreak of World War II, he spent the period 1939 to 1945 in a German prisoner-of-war camp. After a year of wandering in Western Europe, Gałczyński returned home to resume his literary career. He began work as a playwright, inventing an imaginary theatre and troupe of performers (animal and human) and contributing a new installment of *The Little Theatre of the Green Goose* each week to *Przekrój* ("Profile"), the Cracow literary magazine for which he wrote several hundred of these short plays in the next four years.

Originally intended for reading only, *The Green Goose* went unperformed in Gałczyński's lifetime. "The smallest theatre in the world" was by design impossible to stage, or so it seemed according to all known rules of drama. Certainly, by the laws of theatre that had come to prevail in Poland after 1949 – those of socialist realism dictated from the Soviet Union – *The Little Theatre of the Green Goose* was unacceptable as long as the Stalinists reigned. By 1950 Gałczyński had been forced to curb his high spirits and eventually "close" his theatre.

The Little Theatre of the Green Goose was first staged by the Grotesque Puppet Theatre in Cracow in 1955. After the liberalization of the arts brought by the October revolution of 1956, *The Green Goose* gained a permanent place in the theatre and became a force for the creation of the new Polish drama that flourished in the 1960s. "Delight in nonsense has its roots in the feeling of freedom we enjoy when we are able to abandon the straightjacket of logic," writes Freud. A great master of nonsense, Gałczyński offers that feeling of freedom to both readers and theatre-goers.

Earlier versions of these translations appeared in the Special English Language Issue of *Dialogue*, Warsaw, 1969 and in *Twentieth-Century Polish Avant-Garde Drama*, Ithaca, N.Y., 1977.

The Little Theatre of the Green Goose
by
Konstanty Ildefons Gałczyński

Translated by Daniel Gerould

All inquiries concerning performance rights of *The Little Theatre of the Green Goose* should be addressed to: Samuel French, 45 West 25th St., New York, NY 10010, USA

The Little Theatre of the Green Goose Has the Honor of Presenting "A Salvation Army Concert"

In which appear:
BISHOP BURKE, drum
MISS PETIT POOH
JOHNNY BROWN, former alcoholic, trumpet
A CROWD OF THE MORALLY MISGUIDED
and RAIN

Scene: Boston, U.S.A., 7th Street.

BISHOP BURKE, MISS PETIT POOH, and JOHNNY BROWN: (*Beating on the drum, fiddling on the violin, and trumpeting*) Holy-holy-hallelujah!
CROWD OF THE MORALLY MISGUIDED: (*Undergoes a very slight moral rebirth.*)
RAIN: (*Starts to sprinkle.*)
BISHOP BURKE: (*Beating on the drum*) Oh, hell. Brethren. The end of the world is coming. The Gobi fish will come out of the depths of the waters and devour the Rockefeller Institute and the Peace Conference. So too will this fish completely devour the inventors of the atomic bomb and the inventors of the meat grinder. Then the vegetarians will be on the right, the meat caters on the left, and I will be in the middle. Buy my pamphlet, *How I Became a Vegetarian.*
MISS PETIT POOH: (*On the violin*) Holy-holy-hallelujah.
BISHOP BURKE: Along with a color portrait of the Gobi fish, only four dollars. Four dollars. Four dollars. Four dollars. Four dollars.
JOHNNY BROWN: (*Trumpet*) Holy-holy-hallelujah. Holy-holy-hallelujah.
BISHOP BURKE: Thank you. Four dollars. Holy-thank you-hallelujah!
CROWD OF THE MORALLY MISGUIDED: (*Undergoes a total rebirth.*)
RAIN: (*Coming down in buckets.*)
JOHNNY BROWN: (*Every so often pours water out of his trumpet and gazes longingly at the sign in front of the bar, "The Jolly Owl."*)
MISS PETIT POOH: (*By mistake pours water out of a size 12 shoe into the violin.*) Blasted downpour. It's an absolute cloudburst. Boston's

turning into an aquarium. I splash, you splash, he, she, it splashes. We splash, you splash, they splash.

BISHOP BURKE: (*Through the rain and darkness, stopping beating on the drum*) The hell with it all! Well, friends, one more "holy-holy" and we'll call it quits.

CURTAIN

1946

The Little Theatre of the Green Goose Has the Honor of Presenting
"The Drama of a Deceived Husband"
or
"Crushed by the Credenza"

Characters:
A MAN and A CREDENZA

(*The stage represents a small room in which stands the above-mentioned antique three-tiered credenza with a drolly shaped ornamental railing and a cornice with trumpeting cherubs.*)

MAN: "Cogito, ergo sum" – which means, "I think, therefore I am" – said our friend Descartes. But what if I am, if my wife never is. She sits and gossips all day long in a café.

And meanwhile:
    The mushrooms are not marinating,
    The socks aren't getting darned,
    The dust's not being wiped away,
    The beds aren't getting made,
    The fish aren't being scaled,
    The potatoes are not peeled,
    The eggs aren't being boiled,
    The faucets aren't turned off,
    So I stare at the bare wall,
    And swallow bitter tears.

(*Swallows again and again.*)

My only companion, my only friend is this old credenza, witness of all my sufferings and longings. Oh, if you could only speak, old credenza, credenza with your ornamental railing of indeterminate shape and your cornice on which two cherubs blow golden trombones

But I have the impression that credenza's starting to tip again. Pikus probably bit off the leg again. That damned Pikus!

(*With a gesture of despair he straightens the credenza; the credenza falls over and crushes him.*)

MAN: (*From under the credenza*) Oh, this is great! Maybe now my sufferings will finally end. What's that? Aha, that's the jar of horseradish that's come open, and the horseradish is dripping in my eyes. I forgive you, Marie. (*A pause.*)

Marie, where are you right now? At Alice's, maybe? Or perhaps at your favourite café? Or maybe you've enrolled in a course in gliding and are soaring now like a swallow through the clouds high above the commonplace chimney of our house and, as it were, all this vanitas vanitatum? Like a bright spirit you're beyond this earthy vale of tears. While I am underneath the credenza. Marie, I forgive you. And you, credenza, crush me all the way.

CREDENZA: (*in a human voice*) All right, here we go! (*Crushes him all the way.*)

CURTAIN

1949

The Little Theatre of the Green Goose Has the Honor of Presenting "The Atrocious Uncle"

In which appear:
   THE ATROCIOUS UNCLE
   THE UNHAPPY AUNT
   GENERAL VENDETTA

THE ATROCIOUS UNCLE: (*Drips with blood.*)
THE UNHAPY AUNT: Well, what's your latest prank, Aloysius?
THE ATROCIOUS UNCLE: I murdered the Baroness.
THE UNHAPPY AUNT: (*In a hollow voice*) That's your sixth crime so far this week. Aloysius, what's happened to you?
THE ATROCIOUS UNCLE: Boredom. I'm bored.
THE UNHAPPY AUNT: So you're bored, are you? Oh, too bad I'm paralyzed, or I'd braid myself a narcissus wreath and dance you a dance of the South Sea Islands. Remember how in Junction City ...
THE ATROCIOUS UNCLE: Where's our pussycat?
THE UNHAPPY AUNT: It went out on the roof.
THE ATROCIOUS UNCLE: Too bad, I wanted to strangle it. Strangle. Strangle. Boredom.
THE UNHAPPY AUNT: Oh, strangle me, miserable wretch. After all, there's little joy in life for me as it is, since you gouged out my left eye and I'll only see half the spring this year.
THE ATROCIOUS UNCLE: Spring? Spring will come when the general returns.
THE UNHAPPY AUNT: But will he return?
THE ATROCIOUS UNCLE: He'll return, sword in hand. On a white horse. And all the bells will ring. And there won't be any more boredom, only building for the future and the great inspired cry of regeneration. The price of eggs will go down. I'll become district governor of Smolensk. God save the general.
THE GENERAL: (*Doesn't return.*)
THE ATROCIOUS UNCLE: (*Strangles the cat.*)

CURTAIN

1946

The Little Theatre of the Green Goose
Has the Honor of Presenting
A Bloody Drama in Three Acts
With Vinegar
Taken from Life in the Upper Reaches of Academic
High Society
entitled
"Pickled Alive"

In which appear:
GASPARON, the ghastly baron
GASPARINA, the unfaithful baroness
and JEAN ODOROUS, the faithful servant

Act I

Setting: A secret gallery leading to the door of the Baroness' bedroom.

BARON: (*Peeping through the keyhole*) By Jove, Jean, I've had my fill. The Baroness is deceiving me with a full professor. I won't live through the aforementioned, inasmuch as I'm having a moral breakdown. (*Has a moral breakdown, as well as tottering on his feet.*)
JEAN ODOROUS: Courage, my lord. Your fears will soon be laid to rest.
BARON: (*Peeping through the keyhole once more.*) Whew. They already have been.

Act II

Setting: The Baron's library. In the middle of the library a jar of alarming proportions.

BARON: (*Suffering; aside*) If the soul weren't immortal, I'd say my soul had been mortally wounded. Women, women! (*A knock.*) Ontray!
BARONESS: (*Entering*) Don't you want a drink, Joevanny?
BARON: Yes, thanks. (*His teeth chattering.*)
BARONESS: Oh, almighty God! What does that sinister jar mean?

BARON: Ha, ha! You'll find out about all that soon enough. Jean!
JEAN: (*Entering*) Did madam ring?
BARON: Nonsense. Madam didn't ring and will never ring again. Die, faithless woman. (*Aided by Jean, he grabs hold of the Baroness, and they both stuff the latter into the waiting jar, pouring vinegar over the contents.*)

Note: To spare the nerves of the esteemed Public, the remaining phases of the pickling process take place offstage.

Act III

(Conceived in an operatic style)
ARIA OF THE BARONESS IN THE JAR
(in verse)
My career glittered like a star,
Today that star's gone out. For being fickle
The Baron's put me in a jar
And now I'm leading the life of a pickle.

CURTAIN
Falls by mistake, so it goes back up again

ARIA OF THE BARONESS IN THE JAR
(continuation)
My prayers can never alter my fate,
I can't get out from where I've sunk.
Who'd fall in love with me in such a state?
Except maybe some drunk.

1947

The Little Theatre of the Green Goose Has the Honor of Presenting "The Peculiar Waiter"

In which appear:
    THE PECULIAR WAITER
    FIRST CUSTOMER
    SECOND CUSTOMER
    THIRD CUSTOMER

PECULIAR WAITER: What did you have?
FIRST CUSTOMER: Lamb chops.
PECULIAR WAITER: Lamb chops two dollars. No cocktails?
FIRST CUSTOMER: No cocktails.
PECULIAR WAITER: No cocktails five dollars. Any beer?
FIRST CUSTOMER: No beer.
PECULIAR WAITER: No beer six dollars, chops two dollars; that's eight dollars; thank you, sir. (*To the Second Customer.*) You had tongue with horseradish sauce?
SECOND CUSTOMER: No, three eggs scrambled.
PECULIAR WAITER: No tongue with horseradish sauce two-fifty, three eggs scrambled ninety-nine cents, no champagne sixty dollars; altogether that comes to sixty-three dollars and forty-nine cents; thank you, Sir; good-night, Sir.
THIRD CUSTOMER: (*Gets up and pokes a hole in the Peculiar Waiter's head with his oak cane.*)
PECULIAR WAITER: A hole in the head eight-fifty, pork chops two dollars; altogether that comes to ten-fifty; no beer a dollar, so that's eleven-fifty; thank you, Sir; good-night, Sir. Come back again, sir.

CURTAIN

1946

The Little Theatre of the Green Goose Has the Honor of Presenting "The Burial of a War Criminal"

In which appear:
  THE FUNERAL DIRECTOR
  THE GRAVEDIGGERS
    and THE PUBLIC

THE FUNERAL DIRECTOR: Ladies and Gentlemen. In a moment War Criminal No. 8 will be buried. Quiet, please.
THE PUBLIC: Bravo!
THE GRAVEDIGGERS: (*Lower the corpse.*)
THE PUBLIC: Encore!
THE GRAVEDIGGERS: (*Raise the corpse up and let it down again.*)
THE PUBLIC: Encore!!
THE GRAVEDIGGERS: (*As above*)
THE PUBLIC: (*Completely carried away*) Encore!!!!
THE GRAVEDIGGERS: (*Keep giving encores without stopping*)
THE PUBLIC: (*Delighted to have disposed of the war problem, demands further encores.*)

CURTAIN

1946

The Little Theatre of the Green Goose
Has the Honor of Presenting
Act III of an Opera
called
"Judith and Holofernes"

In which appear:
    JUDITH
    HOLOFERNES
    CHORUS
        and TRUMPETERS

JUDITH:
    The day's heat is spent.
    The shadows deep.
    There in his tent
    Holofernes sleeps.
(*She goes into the tent where Holofernes is napping.*)
    And yet how sad it seems!
    My heart has almost stopped.
    Now, head, I'll cut you off.
    Chop.
CHORUS:
    She's cutting off, she's cutting off,
    She's cutting off his head.
    She's cutting off, she's cutting off,
    She's cutting off.
TRUMPETERS: (*Trumpeting*) Ta-ta-ta-ta.
JUDITH:
    The bloody work is ended,
    And joy is mixed with dread,
    Now, head, I've cut you off,
    Oh, Holofernes' head.
CHORUS:
    She has cut off, she has cut off,
    She has cut off his head.
    She has cut off, she has cut off,
    She has cut off.
TRUMPETERS: (*Trumpeting*) Ta-ta-ta-ta.
HOLOFERNES: (*With a missing head*) Wonder how I'll get along now.
    Unless I get used to it.

CHORUS: (*Casts doubt on Holofernes' assertion.*)
  Forsooth, forsooth,
  You dirty dog, forsooth,
  Get used, get used,
  You think that you'll get used?

CURTAIN

1947

The Little Theatre of the Green Goose
Has the Honor of Presenting
With Horror
A Play in Prose and Verse
called
"When Orpheus Played"

Characters:
  MAESTRO ORPHEUS
  and MANY WILD ANIMALS

Motto:
"Orpheus, son of Apollo and the muse Clio, played so beautifully and ardently on his instrument that the wildest animals heard him with emotion and immediately grew tame, so to speak, automatically."
Professor Bączyński,
Mytho- and Angelological Dictionary,
Fourth edition, Lumberville, 1878.

ORPHEUS: (*In a grotto*) Something tells me I feel like playing something. But what to play? Aha, now I know what to play. Well, folks, I'll play "The Turkish March" by Wolfgang Amadeus Mozart. (*Turning to his strings, which are strung on a pocket harp.*)
  Say, strings, what could be finer,
  Than Mozart's "Turkish March" in A minor?
(*The strains of the well-known composition by the talented composer issue forth from the grotto in a flawlessly executed performance.*)
LION:
  When I hear Orpheus play his lyre
  It stirs me to the inmost fiber.
(*Weeps and is morally transformed to such an extent that instead of devouring innocent creatures, he masters with lighting speed the fine art of tailoring and sews Orpheus a winter overcoat.*)
EIGHT TIGERS:
  The way he plays affects us too,
  Friend lion, the same as it does you.
(*Become hairdressers.*)
SCANDALMONGERING OLD HAG:
  Maestro Orpheus, your art
  Finds its way straight to the heart.
(*Licks Orpheus' feet and undergoes a spiritual rebirth.*)

(*In a while the whole neighboring town enjoys the services of the animals, tamed and trained by the playing of Orpheus, son of Apollo and the muse Clio. A certain lion, brother of the tailor-lion, becomes a motorman-lion on the local streetcars; the tigers, on account of their colored coats, decorate the lawns for lack of flowers in winter, wild, towering giraffes are turned into street lights, etc.*)

CURTAIN
comes down, lowered by an anteater

1949

The Little Theatre of the Green Goose Has the Honor of Presenting "The Flood That Failed in Winter"

In which appear:
  NOAH
  NOAH's WIVES
  NOAH's CHILDREN
    and NOAH's ANIMALS

NOAH: Honored guests, friends, and relatives!
ANIMALS: Please make it brief.
NOAH: I'm just about finished. Now, as I've explained to you, our Biblical situation doesn't leave us any way out. As you can see, all the waters have frozen over, which makes the ark an absurdity. Do you all agree that we should turn the ark into a sleigh?
WIVES AND CHILDREN OF NOAH: (*Stamping their feet with cold*) Brrr-brrr! We agree.
NOAH: (*Turns the ark into a sleigh, attaches bells, and the whole group rides off up to Mount Ararat on a sleigh ride.*)

CURTAIN

1947

The Little Theatre of the Green Goose Has the Honor of Presenting A Real-Life Drama called "In the Clutches of Caffeine" or "The Frightful Effects of an Illegal Operation"

In which appear:
ROBERT
ROBERTA, Robert's wife
THE JAMAICA CHARLATAN

(*Scenes I and III represent a villa on the edge of a precipice. Scene II in the Jamaica Charlatan's office.*)

Scene 1

ROBERT: *J'adore le café, J'adore le café*. I love coffee. Drink.
ROBERTA: Robert, stop guzzling down that hideous coffee. You know how terribly bad it is for your heart.
ROBERT: (*With a diabolical gleam in his eyes.*) For what?

Scene 2

ROBERT: Are you the Jamaica Charlatan?
JAMAICA CHARLATAN: Yes, I am. I can change sex and height. I can make hair grow. I can make people younger. I perform miracles. On request I soar through the air as Miss Ophelia in a transformed shape. Specialty, teeth and hearts.
ROBERT: Yank away.
JAMAICA CHARLATAN: What? A tooth?
ROBERT: No. A heart.
JAMAICA CHARLATAN:
   You don't like love, but coffee? Drink!
   Because at last you've found the man
   Who'll cure your heartaches in a wink:
   The famous Jamaica Charlatan.

Just drop ten dollars in the bank.
Thanks. The knives are on the cart.
With a snippety-snip, clinkety-clank;
Whoosh-whish! Good-bye, sweet heart!
(*Takes out Roberts heart. Robert immediately goes out for a cup of coffee.*)

Scene 3

ROBERTA: At last you've come back, darling. There's some marvelous bean soup in the mess hall.
ROBERT: Never. *J'adore le café*. From now on it's going to be nothing but Coffee.
ROBERTA: Oh, that coffee again. You'll ruin your heart completely, Robert.
ROBERT: Oh, not anymore now.
ROBERTA: (*Notices the black hole in the place where Robert normally kept his fountain pen.*) Good heavens, you look strange! Come here, close to me. Kiss me. By Jove, I don't hear your heart beating at all.
ROBERT: And you won't hear it anymore. For only ten dollars I had my heart taken out, and now, I can drink coffee night and day without having to worry about apoplexy. *J'adore le café*. Drink.
ROBERTA: (*Gives him a bucket of coffee.*)
ROBERT: (*Disappointed*)* Coffee doesn't taste good anymore. I don't feel like kissing. It seems you have to put your heart into everything. But now I don't have a heart anymore. And that's why I can't love either coffee or you, Roberta. Then what is life? (*Throws himself over the precipice.*)

CURTAIN

1946

---

* Robert must be played by a consummate actor who can portray Robert's disappointment with all the resources of the art of pantomime (author's note).

The Little Theatre of the Green Goose Has the Honor of Presenting "Miracle in the Desert"

In the principal role:
ALOYSIUS PTARMIGAN
In an episodic role:
A MALE BABY

Setting: Desert, palm trees, camels.

ALOYSIUS PTARMIGAN: Here I am in the desert. No water, no cool shade, not a single co-op. Desert, thy name is hopelessness. But what's that that's making such remarkable sounds under a cactus leaf? Aha, it's a male baby abandoned by a degenerate tourist. By Jove, I'd rather die myself than leave this babe uncared for! Courage, Ptarmigan!
(*Takes the babe by the hand.*)
But how will I feed you, poor little thing? Not a brewery on the horizon, and personally speaking, I'm a man. The only thing left is faith in miracles.
(*He has faith and immediately grows ladies breasts.*)
A miracle! A miracle! Oh, take some refreshment, my babe, and then go to sleep like an angel.
BABY: (*He's a realist and doesn't believe in miracles; starts to cry.*) Aaaaaaaaa ...!
PTARMIGAN: (*Notices that the breasts are there but don't have any nourishment in them; gets upset.*) O-o-o-o-o-o-o-oh ...!
BABY: (*Pulls out a package of powdered milk; takes some refreshment.*)
DESERT, PALM TREES, AND CAMELS: (*Split their sides laughing.*)
PTARMIGAN: I'm leaving, clutching my crumbling faith in miracles in my right hand and my shattered world view in my left.
(*Leaves.*)

CURTAIN
gets caught on a palm tree as it falls

1947

The Little Theatre of the Green Goose Has the Honor of Presenting A Ballet called "The Poet Is in Bad Form"

(*The stage represents the Poet's apartment. On the walls pictures of various things. The Poet's Relatives, both Close and Distant, sit on chairs against the walls. The Poet himself sits at a table, almost entirely buried in a mountain of manuscripts.*)

POET: (*Executes the so-called* pas de quoi, *which is to signify that his writing isn't going too well; he tears up a manuscript; as a sign of protest he pours a bottle of green ink over his head; executes three* pas de quoi, *one leap à rebours, and three* châteaux d'Espagne.)

MOTHER-IN-LAW: (*Executes a gloomy tarantella, which is to signify a certain state of economic anxiety, or – if my son-in-law stops writing, what'll we live on? In addition the mother-in-law executes four* pirouettes à la saucisse *in a more optimistic spirit, or – perhaps my son-in-law will still go on writing.*)

DISTANT RELATIVES: (*Who have been helped out by the Poet with loans, both large and small [in the period of the great outpouring of his creative energy], express, in the form of the so-called* danse macabre, *their grief at the ebbing of his creative energy.*)

POET: (*Totally abandoned by Inspiration, tears out his hair, eyebrows, eyelashes, and other things.*)

CLOSE RELATIVES: (*Wag their heads in three-four time.*)

POET: (*Makes a superhuman effort of will; masters himself; his eyes flash like spring lightning, and behold, inspired works begin to cover the parchment.*)

CLOSE AND DISTANT RELATIVES: (*Joyful dance, a form of can-can and* pas de chose.)

CURTAIN

1950

The Little Theatre of the Green Goose Has the Honor of Presenting A Play About the Life of the Intellectual Elite entitled "Hamlet and the Waitress"

Characters:
  HAMLET, Prince of Denmark
  WAITRESS, that kind of woman
  MAURICE EVANS, no comment
  DEVILISH PETE, a pig

Place: A pub, "At the Sign of the Plucked Eyebrows."
Time: Indefinite.

HAMLET: (*Bass*) What can I have?
WAITRESS: Everything. (*Unfastens her brooch and takes off her shoes.*)
HAMLET: (*Soprano; firmly*) No. We'll put that off till Tuesday. I mean what can I have in the way of something to drink?
WAITRESS: Coffee, tea.
HAMLET: (*Lyric tenor*) Then I'll take coffee. No. Tea. No. Coffee. No. Tea. No. But why not tea? No. Coffee. Coffee. Tea. Tea. Coffee. Coffee. Coffee. Coffee.
(*A pause; dimming of the lights; mezzosoprano.*) Tea!
WAITRESS: But why not coffee?
MAURICE EVANS: But why not tea?
HAMLET: (*Dies from a lack of decision and a twist of the guts at a sharp turn in history.*)
DEVILISH PETE: It's just ghastly. The women are going crazy. (*Writes in firm white chalk on Hamlet's black coffin:* HAMLET IDIOT.)

CURTAIN

1948

The Little Theatre of the Green Goose
Has the Honor of Presenting
A Polish Drama
Of the So-called "Ponderous" Variety
entitled
"He Couldn't Wait It Out"

In which appear:
HE and SHE

Act I

SHE: Do you love me?
HE: I love you.
SHE: And will you always love me?
HE: Always.
SHE: Even if I leave you?
HE: What? (*Has an epileptic fit.*)
SHE: Calm down, baby. For just a minute. While I go to the store. To get your great favorite – hot dogs.
HE: Oh, that's different. Get ten pounds. The night is ours.
SHE: Bye-bye, darling. And will you miss me?
HE: Yes, I'll miss you, dearest. I'll die I'll miss you so much. So come racing right back. Don't torture your turtledove.

Act II

HE: (*Alone*) Waiting's a perfect hell! My feelings are a hurricane! No. I can't stand it any longer. (*He can't stand it any longer, goes cross-eyed, mad, after which he falls over on the floor with a crash and dies from longing.*)

Act III

SHE: (*Without moving*) Oh!
(*She lets the hot dogs fall out of her hands and strews the aforementioned him with hot dogs as though with flowers.*)

CURTAIN

1947

The Little Theatre of the Green Goose Has the Honor of Presenting Its Author Wielding a Terrible Pen "The Tragic End of Mythology"

Characters:
   LEDA, the lawful wife of Tyndareus
   JOVE, a noted sex fiend
   and A FRYING PAN

LEDA: Jove! Ah!
JOVE: (*Grim; with a frying pan hidden in the folds of his chlamys*) What now?
LEDA: Jove, oh, how handsome you were as a swan! How you kissed me! How you kissed me!
JOVE: Well, what of it? That's enough rhapsodizing. What I'd like to know is, Where are the eggs, and how many are there?
LEDA: Here they are, darling. Here. Three. Written out, t-h-r-e-e, just the way it is in all the handbooks on classical mythology. And the sequence of events is the same. First you changed into a swan. Then that night in Acapulco. And in just a minute now our three mythological children, Castor, Pollux, and Helen, will be hatched from the three mythological eggs.
JOVE: (*Very grim, nervously handling the frying pan hidden in the folds of his chlamys*) That's enough! (*Pulls out the frying pan from under his arm, turns on the electric stove, and using the three mythological eggs, whips up some realistic scrambled eggs with chives.*)
LEDA: What have you done, miserable wretch?
JOVE: What the conscience of my Jovian stomach dictated. You're an idiot, Leda. But maybe you'll understand this: we can't expect anything worthwhile from Castor and Pollux, and as for Helen, everybody knows the consequences – the Trojan war. And we've certainly had enough wars. (*Digs into the scrambled eggs.*)

                      CURTAIN
                          falls

1949

The Little Theatre of the Green Goose Has the Honor of Presenting "Principles of the Relay Cure" or the so-called "Transfer Therapy"

Act I

FIRST DOCTOR: What seems to be the trouble?
PATIENT: My foot.
FIRST DOCTOR: Your foot? In that case you'll go down to Clinic F.
PATIENT: Yes, but that's just it, I can't walk.
FIRST DOCTOR: Oh, really? Well then, they'll carry you.

Act II

SECOND DOCTOR: What seems to be the trouble?
PATIENT: My foot.
SECOND DOCTOR: Which one?
PATIENT: The left one.
SECOND DOCTOR: Splendid. Orderly Junebug, carry this patient to Clinic LF.

Act III

THIRD DOCTOR: What seems to be the trouble?
PATIENT: My left foot.
THIRD DOCTOR: Very good, but is it more of a nervous complaint or a physical pain?
PATIENT: Nervous.
THIRD DOCTOR: Wonderful. I'll have you transferred to the clinic for those with nervous disorders of the left foot, or Clinic NLF.

Act IV

PATIENT: My head's starting to ache slightly.
FOURTH DOCTOR: Great. Now we'll finally be able to make a slight improvement in the statistics of the clinic for the mentally ill.

Act V

FIFTH DOCTOR: That patient looks sad. Are you by any chance longing for another life?
PATIENT: Oh, yes, extremely.

Epilogue

(*An elegant carriage from the Rest Institute* ETERNITY-AETERNITAS *pulls up, and the Patient, now liberated from cares, but well stocked with several thousand diagnoses, drives off in the well-known direction.*)

CURTAIN
comes down forever

1947

The Little Theatre of the Green Goose Has the Honor of Presenting "The Seven Sleeping Brothers"

FIRST BROTHER: (*Snores.*)
SECOND BROTHER: (*Snores.*)
THIRD BROTHER: (*Snores.*)
FOURTH BROTHER: (*Snores.*)
FIFTH BROTHER: (*Snores.*)
SIXTH BROTHER: (*Snores.*)
SEVENTH BROTHER: (*Snores horribly.*)

                    CURTAIN

1946

The Little Theatre of the Green Goose Has the Honor of Presenting "Greedy Eve"

In which appear:
 THE SNAKE, ADAM, and EVE

SNAKE: (*Gives* EVE *the apple on a tray.*) Take a bite and give it to Adam.
ADAM: (*Roars*) Give me a bite. Give me a bite.
EVE: (*Eats the whole apple.*)
SNAKE: (*Aghast*) What'll happen now?
ADAM: It doesn't look so good. The whole Bible's a total loss.

CURTAIN

1946

The Little Theatre of the Green Goose Has the Honor of Presenting "Rain"

CHORUS OF PEOPLE WAITING FOR THE BUS: Oh, how boring it is to wait for the bus.
RAIN: (*Begins to pour.*)
CHORUS OF PEOPLE WAITING FOR THE BUS:
Screw this rain.
Screw this waiting.
Screw this bus.
A MAN DRIVING BY IN HIS CAR: (*Gets out of his car in front of the line of people waiting.*) My car's very tiny. My car won't hold all of you. But there's one simple thing I can do: I can get out of my car; I can stand in line; I can wait and get soaked with you.
(*Stands last in line.*)

CURTAIN

1949

The Little Theatre of the Green Goose Has the Honor of Presenting "Lord Hamilton's Night"

In which appear:
LORD HAMILTON
INNKEEPER
and GRANNY

Setting: An inn, "At the Sign of the Gold Owl and Multiplication Table." A windy night in early spring.

INNKEEPER: Goddam. I wanted to close up now. Alas. Here comes that terrible rake Hamilton, with an unsteady gait, holding a Dutch lantern above his head to light his way. We'll have to open up, Granny.
INNKEEPER's GRANNY: (*Opens up.*)
LORD HAMILTON: (*Entering*) Good evening, ghosts. Give me something to drink. Life is a pun, and a pun is nonsense with a double meaning. So I'd like a double whiskey.
INNKEEPER's GRANNY: (*Pours him a drink.*) Here it is, milord.
LORD HAMILTON: (*Pulls out a pistol and shoots pure, innocent GRANNY dead.*)
INNKEEPER's GRANNY: By Jove!
(*Dies.*)
INNKEEPER: I notice that your lordship has taken the liberty of murdering my beloved Granny as a prank. Isn't that too much?
LORD HAMILTON: (*Observing with interest the cloud of smoke above the muzzle of his pistol.*) I don't know. That's up to you. Add grandmother to the bill.
INNKEEPER: (*Adds her to the bill.*)
Wind. Terror.

CURTAIN

1947

The Little Theatre of the Green Goose Has the Honor of Presenting A Meteorological Drama entitled "Family Happiness" or "Watch out for Expletives"

In which appear:
DADDY
MUMMY
GRANDMA
TINY TOT
THUNDER AND LIGHTNING
   and PORPHIRION THE DONKEY

SCENE: A quiet little apolitical, domestic fireside after supper.

GRANDMA: It's so cozy here! (*Adjusts her glasses and darns everything over and over again.*)
MUMMY: (*Looking at Daddy*) Together at last! (*Cries from happiness.*)
TINY TOT: (*Plays with his plush toy dwarf.*)
(*Pause; silence; happiness.*)
DADDY: (*Suddenly*) No, I'm rotting in this bourgeois household! I've had enough! I'm made for better things! I feel I have unlimited potentialities! Hold me back! (*Looking at Grandma and Tiny Tot*) Thunder and lightning! Blast it all!
THUNDER AND LIGHTNING: (*Blasts it all and totally does away with the problem of a quiet little apolitical, domestic fireside after supper.*)
PORPHIRION THE DONKEY: Gracious me, and it all seemed to be getting off to such a nice start!

CURTAIN

1947

The Little Theatre of the Green Goose Has the Honor of Presenting "The End of the World"

GOD: Rrrrrrr. I proclaim the end of the world. Rrrrrrr. (*The whole cosmic contraption starts to come apart.*)

BUREAUCRAT: Rrrrrrr. That's very fine. Rrrrrrr. But where is the relevant document in this case, duly stamped and bearing the number assigned to it up there, which should have been entered in our correspondence file? (*It turns out that there was such a document, but that it got lost, so although the end of the world really does take place in actual fact, officially it doesn't count for anything.*)

CURTAIN
falls optimistically

1947

Other titles in the the Routledge Harwood Polish and East European Theatre Archive series:

Volume 10
The Conspiracy of Feelings
Yurii Olesha
and
The Little Theatre of the Green Goose
Konstanty Ildefons Gałczyński
Edited by Daniel Gerould

Volume 11
A Dream
Felicja Kruszewska
and
An Excursion to the Museum
Tadeusz Różewicz
Edited by Jadwiga Kosicka

Volume 12
Mr Price, Or Tropical Madness and Metaphysics of a Two-headed Calf
Stanisław Ignacy Witkiewicz
Edited by Daniel Gerould

This book is part of a series. The publisher will accept continuation orders which may be cancelled at any time and which provide for automatic billing and shipping of each title in the series upon publication. Please write for details.

For Product Safety Concerns and Information please contact our EU
representative GPSR@taylorandfrancis.com
Taylor & Francis Verlag GmbH, Kaufingerstraße 24, 80331 München, Germany

www.ingramcontent.com/pod-product-compliance
Lightning Source LLC
Chambersburg PA
CBHW052051300426
44117CB00012B/2077